THE KINGFISHER
ILLUSTRATED
DINOSAUR
ENCYCLOPEDIA

Consultant Tim Batty, Curator of The Dinosaur Museum, Dorchester, England

Managing editor Miranda Smith

Coordinating editor Terry Moore

Editors Denise Heal, Laura Marshall

Senior designer Malcolm Parchment

Picture researchers Juliet Duff, Jane Lambert

DTP manager Nicky Studdart

DTP coordinator Primrose Burton

Production manager Caroline Hansell

Additional illustrations

Julian Baker, Richard Bonson, Mike Davis, James Field,
Chris Forsey, Ray Grinaway, Gary Hinks, David Holmes, Mark Iley, Ian Jackson,
Steve Kirk, Terrence Lambert, Bernard Long, Kevin Maddison,
Shirley Mallinson, Bernard Robinson, Tim Slade, Guy Smith, Mike Taylor

KINGFISHER
a Houghton Mifflin Company imprint
222 Berkeley Street
Boston, Massachusetts 02116
www.houghtonmifflinbooks.com

First published in 2001
4 6 8 10 9 7 5 3

3TR/1003/CAC/CLSN/140KMA

LIBRARY OF CONGRESS CATALOGING-IN-PUBLICATION DATA
Burnie, David.
The Kingfisher illustrated dinosaur encyclopedia / by David Burnie.—1st ed.
p. cm.
Includes index.
ISBN 0-7534-5287-1
1. Dinosaurs—Encyclopedias, Juvenile. [1. Dinosaurs—Encyclopedias.] I. Title:
Encyclopedia of dinosaurs. II. Title.

QE861.3 .B87 2001
567.9'03—dc21
2001029350

Printed in China

THE KINGFISHER
ILLUSTRATED
DINOSAUR
ENCYCLOPEDIA

WRITTEN BY DAVID BURNIE

ILLUSTRATED BY JOHN SIBBICK

KING*fISHER*

BOSTON

CONTENTS

Colony-forming graptolites from the Silurian Period, drifting in the sea

Eldonia ludwigi, a primitive echinoderm from the Burgess Shale

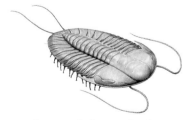

Oryctocephalus matthewi, an early trilobite from the Burgess Shale

Acanthostega (left) and *Ichthyostega* (right and above), two of the earliest four-legged vertebrates

Aysheaia—an ancestor of velvet worms—feeding on sponges during the Cambrian Period

Heleosaurus, a Late Permian reptile

The fossilized skeleton of *Parasaurolophus*, a duck-billed dinosaur

Skeletal muscles of the plant eater *Brachiosaurus*, one of the tallest sauropods

Deinosuchus, a giant crocodilian from the Late Cretaceous, attacking *Corythosaurus*, a duck-billed dinosaur

FOREWORD

This book is about a group of extraordinary animals—the dinosaurs. These reptiles dominated the natural world for more than 160 million years, and from the middle of the 1800s, when the first fossil skeletons were excavated, they have captured the imaginations of generations of people—children and adults alike. Through the patient work of paleontologists and other scientists, we are finding out more and more about these remarkable creatures, the continents they roamed, what they ate, the way they lived.

The work of a paleontologist is painstaking and backbreaking, but sometimes it is unbelievably rewarding. On August 12, 1990, in the Badlands of South Dakota, many miles from any human habitation, I found three articulated vertebrae, some ribs, and a large bone weathering out of a cliff face. I was almost certain that the bones belonged to a *Tyrannosaurus rex*, but I had no idea that the find, "Sue," would prove a record breaker. She is the largest and most complete skeleton of a *Tyrannosaurus* yet discovered—she is 42 feet (12.8m) long and stands 13 feet (4m) high at the hips. *And* she was not alone. She was found with the remains of other tyrannosaurs—a baby, a juvenile, and a young adult.

On May 17, 2000, at the Field Museum in Chicago, Sue's mounted skeleton was unveiled to the world for the first time in 66 million years, and she, like so many dinosaur fossils worldwide, has been attracting millions of visitors ever since. It has taken more than 4.5 billion years for the earth to reach its present state, and we are finding out details about its prehistoric beginnings all the time. Dinosaurs are a significant part of that prehistory. The more we discover about dinosaurs like Sue, the more we find out about the world we live in today.

Sue Hendrickson

Sue Hendrickson

LIFE IN THE DISTANT PAST

If the earth's entire history could be crammed into a single hour, animal life would not appear until the final 15 minutes was well underway. Land animals would make their entrance when the hour had just six minutes left to go, and the Age of Reptiles—one of the most dramatic periods—would run for just over two minutes, when the hour was almost at an end. This chapter looks at the first few minutes of this story and explains some of the processes that have shaped animal life and the evidence that prehistory has left behind.

THE BEGINNING OF LIFE

WHEN EARTH FORMED, ABOUT 4.6 BILLION YEARS AGO, ITS AVERAGE TEMPERATURE WAS AS HOT AS THE SURFACE OF THE SUN. BUT JUST 700 MILLION YEARS LATER LIFE WAS ALREADY UNDERWAY.

Earth is the only place where life definitely exists, although it is possible that elsewhere in the universe other planets have living things of their own. As far as scientists can tell, life arose on Earth through a long series of chemical "accidents" that took place in watery surroundings. Driven by solar and chemical energy, these created the complex substances that form the machinery of all living things.

FOSSIL EVIDENCE

These rocky mounds are stromatolites growing in Shark Bay, Western Australia. They are formed by cyanobacteria (blue-green algae), which are simple microbes that collect energy from sunlight. Cyanobacteria form mounds by trapping sediment, which becomes cemented together. Shark Bay's stromatolites are several thousand years old, but some fossilized stromatolites are 3.4 billion years old—making them among the earliest signs of life on Earth.

WHAT IS LIFE?

Over 99.99999 percent of our planet is made up of inanimate matter—matter that is not alive. Unlike living things, inanimate matter cannot grow or use energy, and it cannot respond to the world around it. Most important, it cannot reproduce. So how did this unpromising starting point generate things that were alive four billion years ago?

The answer, most scientists believe, is by a series of random chemical reactions that took place between carbon-containing substances dissolved in the sea. Some of these reactions formed microscopic bubbles surrounded by oily membranes that contained tiny drops of fluid shielded from the water outside. Others formed substances that could copy themselves by attracting simpler chemicals from their surroundings.

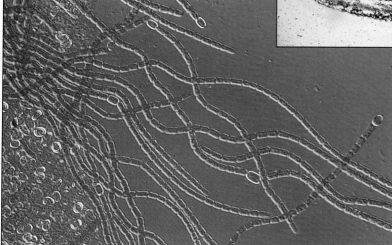

Somehow the two came together and produced the first self-copying cells. When those cells started to use energy, life began.

POWERING UP

The first living things were bacteria. These would have gotten their energy from dissolved chemicals, but as they multiplied, supplies of this chemical food started to dwindle, and a struggle for survival began. This struggle is a feature of life, because living things outstrip their resources. But there are hidden benefits, because this makes living things evolve.

One early result of evolution was that some bacteria evolved a new way of life three billion years ago. They developed the ability to collect energy directly from sunlight. This process, called photosynthesis, was a major step forward, because sunlight delivers energy in vast amounts.

LIFE IN THE FAST LANE

When photosynthesis began, Earth's atmosphere contained nitrogen and carbon dioxide, but hardly any oxygen. Unlike earlier forms of life, photosynthetic bacteria

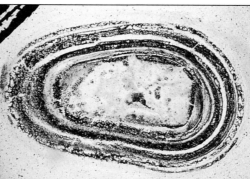

released oxygen as a waste product. The atmosphere's oxygen level began to creep up to 21 percent— today's level.

Oxygen is a highly reactive substance— for many primitive bacteria, a deadly poison—so they had to retreat into mud and sediment where oxygen could not be found. As oxygen became abundant more complex forms of life evolved that used oxygen to their advantage. These organisms could use oxygen to "burn" reserves of fuel stored inside their cells, which meant that they could release energy exactly when they needed it. Life was beginning to speed up.

The first of these "aerobic" organisms were single-celled aquatic microbes, larger than bacteria and much more complex. Called protists, they teem in freshwater and the sea today. But their place at the top was not destined to last, because over a million years ago plants and animals began to evolve.

◁ *This microscopic fossil is from a type of rock called Gunflint Chert, which is found in western Ontario. This rock layer formed about two billion years ago, and it contains some of the earliest known remains of microbes that lived by photosynthesis.*

◁ *The long filaments shown here are strands of* Anabaena, *a present-day cyanobacterium, or blue-green alga.* Anabaena *lives in shallow water and on damp ground. Its way of life is not very different from that of the earliest photosynthetic bacteria.*

◁ *When Earth's crust was newly formed, volcanic eruptions (far left) occurred on a colossal scale. These eruptions actually helped create suitable conditions for life, because they gave off steam, which eventually condensed to form the oceans. They also produced minerals that early bacteria could use as sources of energy.*

EARTH'S FIRST ANIMALS

THE MOST ANCIENT TRACES OF ANIMAL LIFE ARE UP TO ONE BILLION YEARS OLD, BUT THE OLDEST FOSSILS OF ANIMALS THEMSELVES DATE FROM ONLY ABOUT 600 MILLION YEARS AGO, DURING THE VENDIAN PERIOD.

When the first animals evolved, they were soft-bodied and microscopic and lived on or in the seabed. Creatures like these hardly ever fossilized, and the only clues they left behind were indirect ones, such as the remains of burrows and tracks. But despite their tiny size, early animals must have flourished, because they gave rise to Earth's first visible animals: the Ediacarans.

FOSSIL EVIDENCE

Wilpena Pound, a giant bowl of sandstone 10.6 miles (17km) wide, lies in South Australia's Flinders Ranges—the same geological formation where the first Ediacaran fossils were found. The sandstone that makes up these hills formed over 540 million years ago, before animals with hard body parts appeared. The discovery that these rocks can contain animal fossils has changed ideas about evolution.

△ *Measuring less than 0.8 in. (2cm) across, this fossil Ediacaran,* Medusina mawsoni, *looks like the remains of a jellyfish. Many think this animal, or others like it, were the direct ancestors of jellyfish that appeared during the Cambrian Period.*

A CHANCE DISCOVERY

The Ediacarans get their name from the Ediacara Hills, in South Australia. In 1946 an Australian geologist noticed some unusual fossils in slabs of ancient sandstone. Some of the fossils seemed to have been left by corals, jellyfish, and worms, but others were like nothing alive today.

At first the Ediacarans were thought to be animals from the Cambrian Period (page 28)—a time when nature produced a huge burst of animal life, starting about 540 million years ago. But a closer look showed that the Ediacaran fossils were older than this and came from the period now known as the Vendian, immediately before the Cambrian. Until this find the Vendian had seemed to be a biological black hole, containing almost no trace of animal life.

Since the 1940s Ediacaran animals have been found in several different parts of the world, including Greenland, Russia, and Namibia. As more fossils are discovered biologists are trying to decide how these animals lived and what happened to them when the Vendian Period came to a close.

THE EDICARAN WORLD

Unlike most of today's animals, the ones from the Ediacaran did not have heads, tails, or limbs, and they did not have mouths or organs for digesting their food. Instead of pursuing food, they probably absorbed nutrients from the water around them. Some may also have harbored algae— a living partnership that gave them a share of the energy the algae collected from sunlight. Many Ediacarans were fastened to the seabed and looked almost like plants, but others simply lay in the shallows, waiting for nutrients to waft their way.

The plantlike species included *Charnia*, which looked like a feather made of jelly, and *Swartpuntia*, an even stranger animal with four semicircular combs. But the giant of them all was *Dickinsonia*, which could grow to the size of a doormat. Like all other Ediacarans, its body was barely more than paper-thin—essential for an animal that absorbed food through its outer skin.

Compared to the animals that followed them, the Ediacarans led uneventful lives. They had no weapons or defensive armor, nor any other way of resisting attack. There was no need—the Vendian sea was a safe place, because predators had not yet evolved.

A FAILED EXPERIMENT?
Over 50 years after the first Ediacarans were discovered, scientific arguments continue about their place in the animal world. Some scientists have suggested that they were not animals at all, but organisms that were more like today's lichens. Others claim that they

were members of a completely separate kingdom of living things—the Vendobionts —which died out as the Cambrian Period began. Supporters of this theory point to the Ediacarans' strange body plan, which was like a fluid-filled mattress divided by partitions. They claim that Vendobionts were an evolutionary experiment, one that worked successfully until more energetic and aggressive animals appeared in the Cambrian.

MIXED FORTUNES
Because there is so little detailed evidence, neither of these theories has convinced all the experts working on ancient life. Instead, many researchers believe that the Ediacarans were genuine animals, but that they experienced very different fortunes as the Vendian Period approached its final stages. Some gave rise to more familiar animals that became widespread in Cambrian times, but others died out, and their strange features disappeared forever from the animal world.

▽ *This imaginary scene shows a collection of Ediacaran animals from different parts of the world. In the center is* Dickinsonia, *the largest member of the group, which sometimes grew to 3.3 ft. (1m) in length. To its left three featherlike* Charnia *project from the sediment, while a trio of brick-colored* Swartpuntia *are visible farther behind.* Spriggina *—the small animal in front of* Dickinsonia*— resembled a primitive trilobite, although like all Ediacarans, it had no hard body parts.*

HOW ANIMALS EVOLVE

EVER SINCE ANIMALS FIRST APPEARED, THEY HAVE GRADUALLY DEVELOPED DIFFERENT SHAPES AND WAYS OF LIFE. THIS PROCESS—CALLED EVOLUTION—IS A KEY FEATURE OF ALL LIVING THINGS.

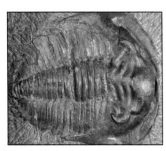
Cambrian trilobite

Ordovician trilobite

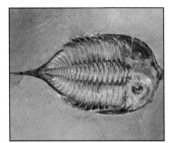
Silurian trilobite

Devonian trilobite

Before the scientific study of fossils began, people believed that the world was created intact, together with all the forms of life that now exist. That would mean, for example, that the world always had two kinds of elephants, about 3,700 kinds of lizards, and about 9,450 kinds of birds. But as fossils of prehistoric animals began to surface, this idea began to look more and more improbable.

ADAPTING TO SURVIVE

Where do prehistoric animals fit into the living world, and why do they no longer exist? Evolution provides the answers. If living things always produced young that were identical to themselves, each different kind—or species—would never change. Young animals would grow up to be exactly the same size and shape as their parents, and they would also behave in exactly the same way. But this is not how nature works. Living things are variable, and they pass on their variations when they breed.

These variations are often tiny, but they can have some far-reaching effects. For example, a lizard that has slightly better-than-average eyesight will be better at catching food. Compared to an average lizard, it is more likely to stay well fed and healthy, which means that it is also more likely to attract a mate and breed. Many of its young will have better-than-average eyesight as well, and they will pass on this variation in their turn. Sharp-eyed lizards will gradually become more common, and eventually better-than-average eyesight will become a feature of the species as a whole. The species will have evolved.

The driving force behind this kind of change is called natural selection, because nature sorts out individuals that have the best features for survival. Natural selection started when life began and has been picking out useful variations ever since.

HOW NEW SPECIES FORM

Evolution works very slowly, so it takes a long time for small variations to have any noticeable effect. (A rare exception to this rule occurs with simple organisms, such as bacteria, because these can breed extremely rapidly.) Over the long term even the smallest variations start to add up, creating major changes in the way animals look and behave. As the generations succeed each other these changes can become so

◁ *Trilobites existed for over 300 million years, and during that time thousands of different species evolved. Each species had its own characteristic shape, with a range of adaptations that suited its particular way of life on the sea floor. Paleontologists are often able to date rocks simply by looking at the trilobites that they contain.*

Phiomia

great that an entirely new species comes into being. Alternatively, differences can make the original species split into more than one line. If these lines remain separate by breeding only among themselves, two or more new species will take the original's place.

In nature different species compete with each other for needed resources, such as food and space to breed. If two species have similar lifestyles, the struggle between them becomes intense. It may continue for centuries or millennia, but the outcome is always the same: one species gets the upper hand; the other declines and may eventually become extinct.

Extinction is a natural feature of life. Usually it occurs very slowly and is balanced by the new species that evolve. But extinction can also occur in sudden waves, when an unexpected change in living conditions wipes out thousands or even millions of species in a short space of time. Many biologists think that we are living through one of these waves today.

TRIED AND TESTED

The study of evolution dates back to the 1800s, with the work of English naturalist Charles Darwin. Darwin collected a mass of evidence showing that evolution occurs, and he identified the driving force behind it. During his lifetime many people imagined that evolution followed a set path, steadily improving living things in the same way that designers improve machines. But today biologists take a different view. The reason

for this is that, unlike a human designer, natural selection cannot plan ahead. Instead, it works like an impartial judge, testing every tiny variation and rejecting any that do not have an immediate use. It cannot select anything that simply might prove useful in the future.

This way of selecting features means that complicated structures, such as eyes, legs, or feathers, have to evolve through a succession of stages and that each of these stages has to bring benefits of its own. Primitive feathers, for example, would have been useless for flight, so they must have served some other function when they first arose. Paleontologists believe that they know what this function was—a discovery that has had a major impact on our understanding of dinosaurs as well as birds (page 132).

Another feature of evolution is that it can never go back to the beginning. Instead, natural selection works with living things as they currently exist, encouraging features that help them make the most of their way of life. But no matter how much living things change on the outside, their bodies still contain the evidence of their long-distant evolutionary past. For paleontologists, this evidence is a treasure trove of information about how living things have evolved.

▽ *Elephants and their relatives arose from a single species, which lived over 40 million years ago. Fossils show that since that time at least 350 different species evolved. From left to right this illustration shows* Phiomia, *which stood about 8.2 ft. (2.5m) tall,* Gomphotherium, *which also had a short trunk and tusks, and* Deinotherium, *which had backward-curving tusks in its lower jaw.* Platebelydon *had lower tusks that worked like a shovel. The imperial mammoth,* Mammuthus imperator, *looked more like a modern elephant, with a long trunk and forward-curving tusks. These animals belonged to several different branches of the elephant line.*

Mammuthus
imperator

Gomphotherium   *Deinotherium*   *Platybelodon*

EVIDENCE FROM THE PAST

BURIED IN SEDIMENT, TRAPPED FOREVER
IN AMBER, OR FROZEN IN ICE—THESE ARE
JUST SOME OF THE WAYS THAT PREHISTORIC
ANIMAL REMAINS HAVE WITHSTOOD
THE TEST OF TIME.

Because most prehistoric animals are now extinct, our knowledge of them comes entirely from the remains they have left behind. With species that died out relatively recently—which in geological terms can mean thousands of years—these remains can include actual body parts, or even entire animals. But with species that lived much further back in time, no body parts are left. Instead, scientists study something else: remains that have literally turned into stone.

△ *This remarkable fossil shows a predatory* Coelophysis *with the remains of a young* Coelophysis *in its stomach. Rare finds like these give an insight into how prehistoric animals behaved.*

THE PAST PRESERVED

When an animal dies, its remains rarely stay in one piece for long. On land scavengers soon home in on the corpse and tear off flesh and bones. Insects lay their eggs in the remains, producing maggots that burrow through what is left. Anything left behind is broken down by bacteria, the most useful natural recyclers. Within days,

This enormous egg—carefully pieced together from broken fragments—was laid by Aepyornis, *a giant flightless bird that lived in Madagascar until perhaps 500 years ago. Although* Aepyornis *is extinct, its eggs are still occasionally found on the island, usually when heavy rain reveals them by washing away the soil. The oldest specimens are fossilized, but this one consists of original shell.*

or weeks if the weather is cold or dry, all that is left is a few scattered bones.

On rare occasions an animal's body is preserved. If the corpse is smothered by something that excludes air, such as volcanic ash or seabed sediment, scavengers and decomposing bacteria are not able to do their work. The corpse remains intact and gradually disappears as further layers of sediment or ash build up. The remains may then be fossilized (pages 18–19)—the ultimate form of preservation, because it can save the shape of living things for several billion years.

STICKY MOMENTS

For biologists interested in the earth's past, fossils are by far the most useful kind of evidence. But prehistoric animals and plants can also be preserved in other ways. When an unlucky insect or small animal encounters a blob of sticky resin oozing from a tree, it can become trapped and then enveloped, sealed inside a transparent tomb, which hardens as it dries. The animal's internal organs decompose, but its outer structure is preserved. Resin itself can fossilize, turning into a glassy substance called amber. Some beads of amber, and the animals locked up inside them, are over 50 million years old.

Resin is not a hazard for large animals, but sticky asphalt, or tar, is. This natural substance seeps up to the surface of the ground, creating treacherous pools that can engulf an animal that ventures across it. The animal becomes impregnated with oily fluids from the tar, which make it very hard for decomposers to attack its remains. The flesh gradually breaks down, but the original unfossilized bones often remain. These relics have been found in several parts of the world, but the most famous is Rancho La Brea, in California. Here an incredible variety of animals has been preserved from Ice Age times (page 212).

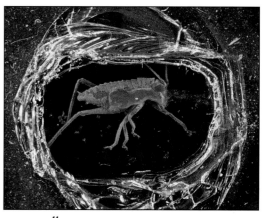

▷ *Trapped in amber, this grasshopper, found in Russia, is about 40 million years old.*

STOPPING THE CLOCK

Some kinds of preservation stop the clock for thousands of years. Mummification is one of these. When a corpse becomes mummified, it dries out completely, which prevents it from bacterial attack. In nature such remains are usually found in deserts and dry caves. The ancient Egyptians used artificial mummification to preserve their dead.

Being frozen is another way of putting decay on hold. In parts of the world such as northern Siberia, where the ground is permanently frozen, remains of Ice Age mammals are often preserved in this way.

▽ *A 10,000-year-old baby mammoth is lifted from frozen ground in northern Russia. The mammoth has been flattened by the weight of the ice above it, but it is completely preserved.*

HOW FOSSILS FORM

FOR A DEAD ANIMAL TO TURN INTO A FOSSIL, CIRCUMSTANCES HAVE TO BE EXACTLY RIGHT. MANY ANIMALS BEGIN TO FOSSILIZE, ONLY TO DISAPPEAR WITHOUT A TRACE.

The word "fossil" originally meant any rock or mineral that was dug up out of the ground. Today it means something much more precise: the remains of plants or animals, which have been preserved in the earth's crust. Unlike the original remains, fossils are tough, and they are also chemically stable, which means that they can survive for incredible lengths of time. Most fossils are at least 10,000 years old, but some date back to the very early days of life on Earth.

FOSSIL EVIDENCE

As well as preserving animals, fossils can also preserve traces that they leave behind. These traces include footprints—like these dinosaur prints from Utah—and also burrows, leftover food, stomach stones (or gastroliths), and fossilized droppings (or coprolites). Trace fossils are interesting because they reveal details of animal behavior, but matching them up with their makers is often a difficult task.

DEAD AND BURIED

The process of fossilization begins when something dies and is quickly covered up, for example by sediment or by an avalanche of underwater mud. Sediment consists of very fine particles, which form a soft blanket over the remains. This blanket protects the remains from scavengers, and it also keeps oxygen out, making it hard for microbes to break down the remains in the normal way.

In many cases this is where the story ends, because waves and currents often disturb remains in water, and wind and rain do

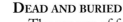

△ *Ammonites and their relatives often formed fossils because they had hard shells and because they lived in shallow seawater—an ideal environment for being buried after death. Like trilobites, their detailed anatomy changed as they evolved, and this allows them to be used as a fossil calendar to determine the age of particular layers of rock.*

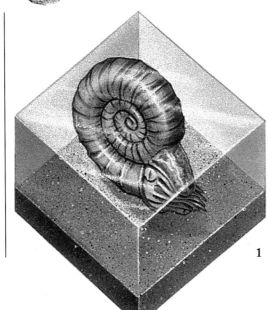

1

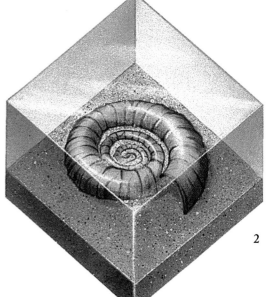

2

the same on land. But if the dead animal lies undisturbed for long enough, more sediment builds up above it. This burial may take place at a rate of just a few millimeters a year, but as time goes by the stage is set for fossilization to begin.

TURNED TO STONE
Hidden away beneath the surface, the minerals that make up any hard body parts, like bones and shells, often dissolve and recrystallize, becoming harder than before. Alternatively underground water may seep through the body parts, dissolving their minerals and washing them away. New minerals are deposited, a process that is often described as turning to stone. These changes occur very slowly, and the remains keep their original shape.

As sediment continues to pile up, the remains become even more deeply buried. Time and increasing pressure do the rest, turning the remains into a fossil and the sediment around it into solid rock.

BACK TO THE SURFACE
Even at this stage things can go wrong. During the thousands or millions of years that it takes a fossil to form, the rock around it may change. The layers may buckle and bend, while extreme pressure may crush the fossil flat. Heat is another factor. If too much warmth reaches the rock from the crust below, the rock may partly melt, and any fossils that it contains will be destroyed. If a fossil manages to escape these hazards, it then has to resurface to be found. This occurs when sedimentary rock is eroded, usually by wind or rain. Then someone has to find the fossil before it falls away from the surrounding rock, breaks up, and finally disappears.

GAPS IN THE RECORD
Because fossilization is so chancy, the earth's fossil record gives a patchy view of prehistoric life. Some animals, such as trilobites and ammonites, fossilized in huge numbers because they had hard shells or body cases and because they lived on the seabed. In the case of trilobites, these animals grew by shedding their skins. Each shed skin formed a perfect trilobite replica, which could also turn into a fossil.

But for some groups—even ones that had bones—fossilization was an uncommon event. This is particularly true of early primates and other mammals that lived in trees. When they died, their bodies dropped to the ground, where scavenging animals fed on them, scattering the remains. Fossil hunters occasionally discover solitary bones or teeth, but complete skeletons are very rare.

◁ *A fossilized* Archaeopteryx, *one of the earliest birds. Unusually, this contains the outline of feathers. Soft body parts usually disappear during fossilization.*

▽ *The diagram below shows typical steps in fossilization.*
1 *An ammonite sinks to the seabed, where it dies.*
2 *The ammonite's shell rests on the seabed, where it is soon covered by fine particles of sediment that drift down from the water above.*
3 *During a process known as diagenesis, the shell's minerals are altered and replaced.*
4 *Further layers of rock form above the fossil.*
5 *Geological movements tilt the rock layers, tipping the fossil onto its edge. Erosion gradually exposes the fossil at the surface.*

3

4

5

STUDYING FOSSILS

WITHOUT FOSSILS OUR KNOWLEDGE OF THE EARTH'S LIVING PAST WOULD STRETCH BACK ONLY A FEW THOUSAND YEARS. BUT WITH THEM SCIENTISTS CAN INVESTIGATE THE ANIMALS THAT LIVED FAR BACK IN TIME.

Fossils are fascinating objects, which explains why many people enjoy collecting them. For paleontologists, the scientists who study the earth's living past, they are also a crucial source of information. They reveal when and how animals lived, what they ate, and sometimes how they reproduced. They also show how different species were linked by evolution. Gathering this information starts with fossil hunting, and it ends when a specimen is cleaned, studied, and assembled and ready to go on view.

△ *These sedimentary rocks at Ghost Ranch, New Mexico, are rich in dinosaur fossils. The red rock was laid down during the Triassic, when the Age of Reptiles began.*

▷ *Here fossilized bones of an allosaur are being removed at Utah's Dinosaur National Monument. Care is taken to prevent fossils from breaking.*

FOSSIL-BEARING ROCKS

Fossil finding is partly a matter of luck and partly a matter of knowing where fossils are likely to be found. It is necessary to be able to recognize the three main types of rock because two of them never contain fossils. The first fossil-free type, igneous rock, includes granite and basalt—rocks that are crystalline and very hard. They develop from molten rock, or magma, which obliterates the remains of any living things. The second type, metamorphic rock, includes marble and slate. These rocks have been transformed by pressure or heat so that any fossils they may have contained will have been destroyed. The third category, sedimentary rock, includes limestone, sandstone, and chalk. Sedimentary rocks are always laid down in layers—a key feature of all fossil-finding sites.

SEARCHING THE GROUND

Some of the world's most interesting fossils have been discovered in places where sedimentary rock is quarried or mined. Many fossils of flying reptiles have come from quarries in Germany, and some of the largest sauropod fossils have been discovered in quarries in the United States. Many other fossils are found by amateurs and professionals searching rocky outcrops where remains have been brought to the surface by erosion. These outcrops include the dry, flat-topped hills in desert areas and coastal cliffs where the rock is undermined by the sea. The softer the rock, the faster it erodes and the more quickly fossils are exposed.

Sometimes fossils are intact when they are found, but wind or rain often separate skeleton bones. Real skill is needed to work out how the bones may have moved and where the rest of the skeleton is likely to be. This kind of hunt often leads up slopes of crumbling rock until the parent material is spotted high above.

UP AND AWAY

Once a fossil has been found,
it is usually extracted so that it can be taken away and studied. For something as small as a trilobite, this can involve little more than a few taps with a hammer to free it from the surrounding matrix or bedrock. But when the fossil is a complete dinosaur skeleton, with individual bones that may be over 3.3 ft. (1m) long, removing the fossil is a major operation that may take several years.

One of the difficulties with this kind of work is that fossilized bones often break up once they are exposed to rain and sunshine. To keep them intact, the bones are wrapped in jackets of quick-setting plaster before they are carried or winched away.

BACK IN THE LAB

Once a fossil has arrived in the lab,
it often needs further work so that it can be fully revealed. Delicate specimens, such as insects or small fish, are cleaned using metal probes, brushes, and machines that resemble dentists' drills. The specimen may also be dipped in a bath of acetic acid, the substance that gives vinegar its sharp smell. This loosens any surrounding rock, which eventually falls away. Fragile bones are hardened by treating them with a plastic, which holds any loose fragments in place.

When the fossil has been cleaned and treated, the process of studying it can begin. The tiniest irregularities or marks can reveal important details, so anything that looks unusual is given a closer look, sometimes with a microscope. This kind of work often resembles forensic science, and in some cases the examination turns up tooth marks or fractured bones, showing how the animal met its end.

Paleontologists can also use medical scanners—a technique that allows them to look at the bony structures beneath the surface. This new way of studying fossils has been used with several kinds of dinosaurs to investigate their brain size (page 129) and to try to work

out whether or not they were warm-blooded (page 148).

JOINING UP

Museums have a limited amount of space, so many fossils end up in storerooms where they can be examined by experts carrying out research. The most important and impressive fossil specimens—particularly of dinosaurs and prehistoric mammals—are reassembled to show what they would have looked like in real life. This process, called articulation, involves arranging the bones so that they are in the correct position and then supporting the entire skeleton so that it does not collapse. Articulation is a complex operation, and even the experts can make mistakes. During the 1800s, for example, the great American fossil hunter Edward Drinker Cope put the skull of the marine reptile *Elasmosaurus* on the end of its tail!

△ *Before large bones can be removed, they have to be channeled out of the surrounding bedrock (top left). The bones are then covered with a protective layer of plaster before being raised with a pulley. Once in the laboratory (left) the plaster is removed. Here the skull of a large allosaur is being examined.*

△ *Laid out on a laboratory bench, the fossilized remains of a plesiosaur are examined by two paleontologists. The fossil was found near Coober Pedy, a mining town in Australia, and its pink color comes from a form of silica found in that part of the world.*

▷ *These six views of the earth show how the continents have moved during the last 245 million years. This part of our planet's history has been dominated by the breakup of Pangaea, the supercontinent that existed when the Age of Reptiles began. Until about 100 million years ago today's southern continents were joined to form a giant fragment of Pangaea called Gondwana, which slowly broke apart.*

CONTINENTS ON THE MOVE

EVERY YEAR SOME OF THE WORLD'S CONTINENTS DRIFT FARTHER APART, AND OTHERS CREEP CLOSER TOGETHER. THESE MOVEMENTS HAVE CHANGED THE FACE OF THE EARTH.

When continental drift was first suggested, nearly 100 years ago, most geologists found it impossible to believe. But today continental drift is an accepted scientific fact, and it is not only continents that are on the move—the earth's entire outer crust is in motion. New oceans open up and force continents apart, and old oceans disappear as continents collide. Because continents carry their wildlife with them, these changes have had a tremendous effect on animal evolution.

ONE WORLD
Today there are seven continents scattered unevenly across the face of the globe. A journey from North America to Europe or from Africa to Australia involves crossing thousands of miles of open sea. But 245 million years ago, at the start of the Age of Reptiles, the world could hardly have

looked more different. All the earth's land was joined together to form a single supercontinent called Pangaea, and the rest of the globe was covered by the vast Panthalassic Ocean. In theory an animal could have walked around the world as long as it could negotiate the mountains and rivers in its way.

Continental drift started when dry land first formed, a time millions of years before Pangaea came into being. Little is known about the continents for most of that time, but it is clear that they also drifted and that giant supercontinents formed several times. One of these ancient landmasses, called Pannotia, existed during the Vendian Period, about 650 million years ago. It broke apart after about 100 million years, creating the separate pieces from which Pangaea was made.

JOINING UP
Continents move at the rate of just an inch or so each year, which adds up to only a tiny distance during an animal's lifetime. Even in the lifetime of an entire species, the positions of the continents barely change. But over millions of years the effects of this movement can be great. It can split up some groups of animals as continents separate and bring others together when they collide.

South America is a perfect example of how this can affect animal life. Until about three million years ago it was an island—one that had been cut off from the rest of the world for nearly 100 million years. During this long period of isolation it

BRIDGES ACROSS THE SEA

Continental drift also shapes the world's climate. It can do this by altering the path of ocean currents, which deliver warm water from the tropics to other parts of the world. Drifting continents also control the world's ice cover, because ice caps can only form over land. If there are no continents near the poles, the polar sea may freeze, but deep ice caps do not form.

For animals the earth's ice cover is important. The more ice there is in ice caps, the cooler and drier the world's climate becomes. At the same time, the world's sea levels fall, because so much of the world's water is in a frozen form. If the sea level falls far enough, it exposes parts of the seabed, and allows animals to travel between nearby continents without leaving dry land. This happened during the last Ice Age, when animals traveled from Asia to North America across the floor of the Bering Sea.

◁ *This map shows how low sea levels allowed animals (and people) to travel from Asia to North America toward the end of the last Ice Age. The dark brown areas show dry land as it exists today; the light brown areas show regions of the seabed that were dry land in Ice Age times.*

developed a wide range of unique animals, including some strange marsupials and the largest rodents that have ever lived. But when South America collided with North America, animals could move between the two continents, and many of South America's native mammals found themselves losing out in the struggle to survive. Three million years on, however, signs of South America's island past are not hard to find—its mammals and birds still include many families that do not exist anywhere else on Earth.

PARTING COMPANY

Further back in time continental drift had an even bigger impact on the way reptiles evolved. When the Age of Reptiles began, Pangaea still existed, so many families of reptiles were found over huge areas of the earth. But after Pangaea split up, some groups evolved in particular parts of the world. One example of these local reptiles was the ceratopsids—a group of armored dinosaurs that were restricted to North America. Another group was the segnosaurs —a little-known family whose remains have been found only in Asia and the Far East.

▽ *Continental drift explains why the remains of some prehistoric land animals can be found in widely scattered regions of the world. The map below shows fossil finds of* Lystrosaurus, *which lived across much of Pangaea over 220 million years ago. After it became extinct its home was broken up by continental drift.*

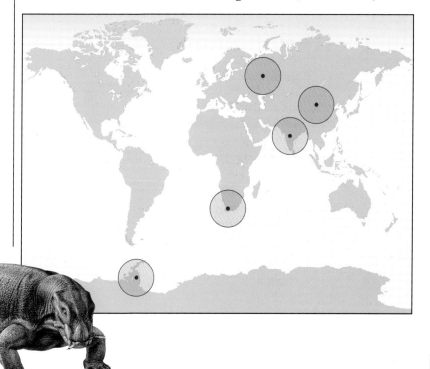

▷ Lystrosaurus *was a mammal-like reptile that lived in the Late Permian and Early Triassic Periods.*

SETBACKS AND DISASTERS

THE FOSSIL RECORD SHOWS THAT LIFE ON EARTH IS A HAZARDOUS AND UNPREDICTABLE BUSINESS. ON SEVERAL OCCASIONS HUGE NUMBERS OF SPECIES HAVE BEEN WIPED OUT IN RELATIVELY SHORT SPACES OF TIME.

Extinction is a natural feature of life on Earth, and it normally happens at a slow and rather unsteady rate. But from time to time external events can trigger off extinctions on a truly colossal scale, and life can take several million years to recover. At least five mass extinctions have taken place in the distant past, with many smaller waves of extinction between them. Each one has rocked the living world and changed the course of animal evolution. The most famous extinction wiped out the dinosaurs, but even greater catastrophes hit animal life further back in time.

TRIGGERING A CRASH

Mass extinctions are extremely rare and are spaced millions of years apart. Abrupt changes in the fossil record show that the last one occurred 66 million years ago, and the previous one happened over 140 million years before that. But although geologists can say when these catastrophes struck, deciding exactly what triggered them is a much more difficult matter.

In the case of the Cretaceous extinction, which swept away the dinosaurs, the most likely explanation is the sudden impact of a meteorite from space (page 204). Meteorite impacts happen all the time, but most of them involve small objects that either burn up in the earth's atmosphere or reach the ground but do little harm. The one that arrived 66 million years ago was a deadly exception—its explosive crash landing obliterated huge areas of natural habitats, and brought the Age of Reptiles to an end.

WHEN LIFE GETS TOUGH

The Cretaceous extinction seems to have been exceptional, and no convincing evidence of giant meteorite strikes has been found for earlier mass extinctions.

Ordovician mass extinction 438 million years ago
Likely cause: climate change
50% of all species wiped out, mainly in the seas

Devonian mass extinction 360 million years ago
Likely cause: climate change
40% of all species wiped out

Permian mass extinction 245 million years ago
Likely causes: volcanic activity, climate change, formation of Pangaea
70% of all land species wiped out

Triassic mass extinction 208 million years ago
Likely cause: climate change
45% of all species wiped out

Cretaceous mass extinction 66 million years ago
Likely causes: meteorite impact, volcanic eruptions
45% of all species wiped out

Vendian 650–540 m.y.a.
(Late Precambrian)

Cambrian
540–505 m.y.a.

Ordovician
505–438 m.y.a.

Silurian
438–408 m.y.a.

Devonian
408–360 m.y.a.

Carboniferous
360–286 m.y.a.

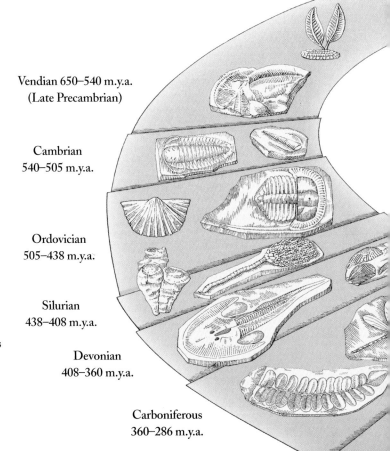

Instead, most experts believe that these biological disasters were caused by natural processes taking place on Earth.

Volcanic eruptions have a lethal effect on almost all forms of life, and there is plenty of evidence from ancient lava flows that they were more common and more violent in the past. Changes in sea level have more subtle effects, but in the long term they can be almost as deadly. When sea levels are high, the world's continental shelves are flooded, creating shallow seas that are rich habitats for marine life. When levels fall again, these shallow seas disappear, along with many of their animal inhabitants. Sea levels fell to record low levels 245 million years ago and probably played a part in the mass extinction at the end of the Permian Period—the greatest setback for life ever known (page 56).

THE SIXTH EXTINCTION?
Climate change is a factor that we are all too familiar with today. In the past the main danger to life was global cooling rather than global warming, but any rapid change in weather patterns in either direction can interfere with plant life and make it harder for animals to find food. Today, there is a final factor to be added to the list: the spiraling rate at which humans use up resources and space. Many biologists think that this is now triggering a sixth mass extinction—one that is caused not by natural events, but by ourselves.

◁ *Immense lava flows, covering hundreds of thousands of square miles, are evidence of huge bursts of volcanic activity in prehistory.*

△ *Climate change, ice formation, and changes in sea levels are connected factors that may have triggered off waves of extinctions.*

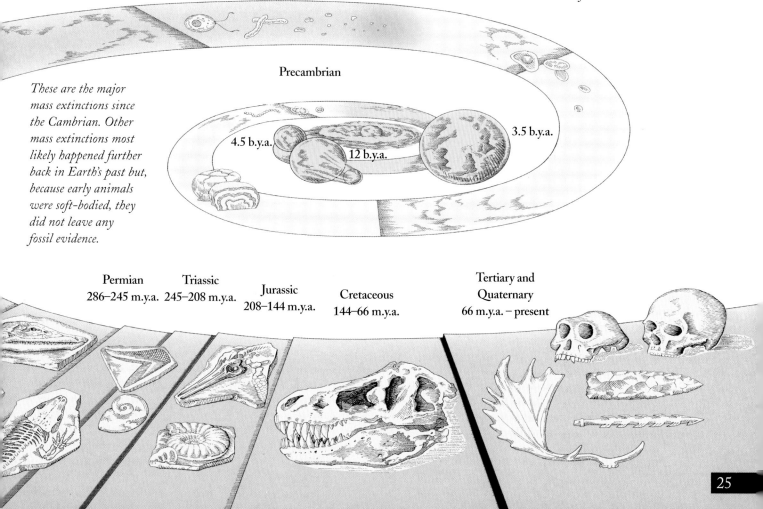

These are the major mass extinctions since the Cambrian. Other mass extinctions most likely happened further back in Earth's past but, because early animals were soft-bodied, they did not leave any fossil evidence.

Precambrian

4.5 b.y.a.   12 b.y.a.   3.5 b.y.a.

Permian 286–245 m.y.a.   Triassic 245–208 m.y.a.   Jurassic 208–144 m.y.a.   Cretaceous 144–66 m.y.a.   Tertiary and Quaternary 66 m.y.a. – present

DIVIDING UP TIME

One way to study the earth's past is to split it into equal intervals—billions of years, for example. But instead of doing this, geologists divide it into intervals that can be seen in layers of sedimentary rock. These layers have built up over millions of years, and they form a permanent record of the earth's past, complete with fossils of plants and animals that were alive when the rock was formed. The boundaries between the layers mark times when conditions on the earth changed rapidly. The changes altered the type of rock that was laid down, and they often made many existing forms of life extinct. The table below shows the names of these intervals, or layers, with the most recent times at the top, working backward into the past. The largest intervals—eons—are divided into smaller ones called eras and periods. These, in turn, are often divided into epochs (only the most recent epochs are shown here). The dates shown for each time interval are approximate. M.Y.A. = million years ago and Y.A. = years ago.

EON	ERA	PERIOD	EPOCH	DATES
PHANEROZOIC	CENOZOIC	QUATERNARY	Holocene Pleistocene	0–10,000 Y.A. 10,000–1.6 M.Y.A.
		TERTIARY	Pliocene Miocene Oligocene Eocene Paleocene	1.6–5.3 M.Y.A. 5.3–23 M.Y.A. 23–36 M.Y.A. 36–58 M.Y.A. 58–66 M.Y.A.
	MESOZOIC	CRETACEOUS		66–144 M.Y.A.
		JURASSIC		144–208 M.Y.A.
		TRIASSIC		208–245 M.Y.A.
	PALEOZOIC	PERMIAN		245–286 M.Y.A.
		CARBONIFEROUS		286–360 M.Y.A.
		DEVONIAN		360–408 M.Y.A.
		SILURIAN		408–438 M.Y.A.
		ORDOVICIAN		438–505 M.Y.A.
		CAMBRIAN		505–540 M.Y.A.
PRECAMBRIAN	PROTEROZOIC	VENDIAN PRE-VENDIAN		540–650 M.Y.A. 650–2,500 M.Y.A.
	ARCHAEAN HADEAN			2,500–3,800 M.Y.A. 3,800–4,600 M.Y.A.

THE AGE OF ANCIENT LIFE

Lasting over 350 million years, the Paleozoic Era, meaning "ancient life," was a momentous time in the animal world. It started in the Cambrian Period with a surge of evolution that has still not been fully explained. At this stage in Earth's history animal life was confined to the seas, but as the era continued some animals made the transition to dry land. By the late stages of the Paleozoic, reptiles and mammallike animals appeared, but the era ended with the greatest mass extinction that the world has ever known.

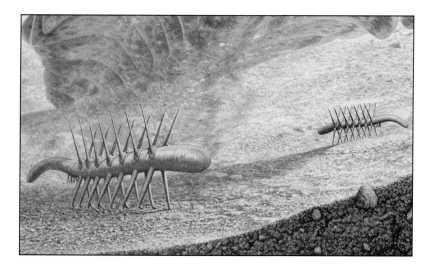

CAMBRIAN PERIOD

BEGINNING ABOUT 540 MILLION YEARS AGO, IN AN EXPLOSIVE BURST OF EVOLUTION, THIS DISTANT PART OF THE EARTH'S PAST SAW THE APPEARANCE OF THE FIRST ANIMALS WITH HARD BODY PARTS.

Because the Cambrian Period was so far back in time, little is known about how the earth looked. There was one major continent and several smaller ones, but for animal life the habitable world lay in the sea. During Cambrian times the climate was warm, and sea levels rose, flooding large areas of low-lying land. These shallow seas created ideal conditions for new kinds of animal life, ones reinforced by shells, body cases, or internal skeletons. These all fossilize easily, so unlike earlier soft-bodied animals, Cambrian animals left a vast store of remains.

▷ *The Cambrian Period was known as the Age of the Trilobites because these animals played such an important part in seabed life. Here several species of trilobites crawl over an ocean floor studded with vaselike archaeocyathan sponges, while jellyfish drift overhead. Most trilobites had well-developed eyes, but* Acadagnostus *(the small species in the foreground) was blind and could roll up in a ball for self-defense.* Paradoxides *(the large trilobite in the center) was usually 8 in. (20cm), but could be 3 ft. (1m) long.*

SHELLS AND SKELETONS

Fossils show that Cambrian animals evolved hard body parts relatively quickly, over a period of perhaps 20 million years. A question that puzzles biologists is why this happened, when animals had been soft-bodied for so long. One possibility concerns the earth's atmosphere. Because of the work of cyanobacteria and algae (pages 10–11), the air's oxygen level had been rising steadily. By the time the Cambrian Period began, it may have been high enough for animals to lead more energy-intensive lives. Extra oxygen would have helped animals to "burn" more food, giving them energy to build new body parts, such as shells and flexible cases.

WHY BE TOUGH?

Animals evolve new features only if they are useful, so these new body parts must have served some essential purpose. For stationary animals there were advantages to growing hard body parts. For example, spongelike animals called archaeocyathans lived by filtering tiny particles of food from the Cambrian seas. They developed internal skeletons, which allowed them to grow a few millimeters off the seabed. Although not a great height, it would have been better for collecting food.

For animals that moved around, a hard covering could be useful in different ways. For Cambrian mollusks a shell, or exoskeleton, provided a mobile shelter that could be used in case of attack. It also acted as an anchor for the soft body parts to develop. For arthropods—which included trilobites and other animals with jointed limbs—hard parts played two separate roles. Their covering, a body case made of separate plates, provided protection, but because it could bend, it also helped them move.

THE CAMBRIAN EXPLOSION

The Cambrian Period saw a huge expansion in animal life—the evolutionary equivalent of the Big Bang. These new animals included some that did not survive beyond the end of the Cambrian, such as those that were first identified as fossils in the famous Burgess Shale (pages 32–35). The Cambrian Period also produced all the main animal groups that are alive today, including the chordates, the group to which we belong.

Known as the Cambrian explosion, this astonishing burst of evolution is difficult to explain. Nothing like it has happened since, so why did it take place? Scientists do not know, but many ideas have been put forward. One is that the explosion was not quite as explosive as it seems. According to this theory many different kinds of animals may have existed before the start of the explosion, but if they were soft-bodied, they would have left few traces. Many scientists believe that this is true. They also think that the Cambrian explosion did happen, although not quite as abruptly as it first seemed. It may have been triggered by changes in oxygen levels or in the layout of the seabed. Or life may have reached a critical point, triggering off a chain reaction in which many new body types were formed.

THE AGE OF ANCIENT LIFE

CAMBRIAN ANIMALS

Although Cambrian animals lived in the sea, few of them were creatures of open water. Instead, animal life hugged the seabed. Worms burrowed their way through the sediment, while snaillike mollusks crept across the surface, feeding on decaying remains. Trilobites also crawled across this surface layer, sometimes leaving telltale tracks that later became fossilized. The water itself was the territory of the fast movers of the Cambrian world: animals such as *Anomalocaris* (pages 32–33) and also—scientists have recently discovered—some of the earliest vertebrates.

△ *Brachiopods, or lampshells, became widespread in the Cambrian. These animals have shells like cockles and other bivalves, but they often grow on stalks.*

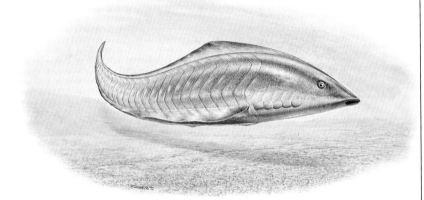

△ Myllokunmingia *sucked up food through its tiny, jawless mouth. This protofish had a skeleton of flexible cartilage.*

▷ *Some Cambrian mollusks, such as* Pleurotomaria *(center), had spiral shells—a strong design that has lasted until the present day.*

▷ *This fossil-rich rock from Australia shows the remains of spongelike archaeocyathans that date back 500 million years to Cambrian times.*

VERTEBRATES AND INVERTEBRATES

Biologists divide the animal world into two overall groups—the vertebrates and invertebrates. Vertebrates are animals that have backbones, and invertebrates are animals that do not. Today vertebrates include all of the largest and fastest animals, but invertebrates are far more varied and much more common, making up about 97 percent of all animal species on Earth.

Invertebrates were undoubtedly the first animals to evolve. Fossils of Ediacaran invertebrates, for example, date back more than 50 million years before the Cambrian began (pages 12–13). During the Cambrian Period a huge range of hard-bodied invertebrates appeared, including sponges and their relatives, arthropods, mollusks, and look-alike animals called brachiopods. But the group the vertebrates belong to, the chordates, is more ancient than was thought.

The first chordates would have been soft-bodied, so have left very few remains. But when chordates began to develop hard body parts made of cartilage and bone, the fossil record becomes more clear. In 1999 scientists in China announced that they had found two fossilized vertebrates in rocks 530 million years old—close to the time the Cambrian Period began. These two animals, named *Myllokunmingia* and *Haikouichthys*, are the world's oldest known fossil fish. Measuring less than 1.2 in. (3cm) long, they were a step along the evolutionary road that was to lead to amphibians and reptiles, including the giants of the dinosaur age.

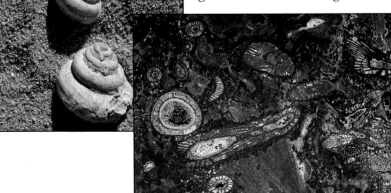

△ *This cross section shows a reef from the Early Cambrian, 535 million years ago. A variety of archaeocyathan sponges are growing on the reef's surface. In crevices below, tracks reveal the presence of small animals hiding away for safety.*

1. **SURFACE LAYER OF LIVING CYANOBACTERIA**
2. **BRANCHING ARCHAEOCYATHAN**
3. **RADIOCYATHAN**
4. *CHANCELLORIA*
5. *OKULITCHICYATHUS*
6. **ARTHROPOD TRACKS**
7. **CEMENTED REEF BASE**

SPONGES ON A REEF

In Cambrian times, just as today, the shallow seabed was often carpeted with life, much of it fixed permanently in place. The most ancient of these seabed dwellers were cyanobacteria—microorganisms that first appeared over 3 billion years ago. Just like their distant ancestors, many Cambrian cyanobacteria collected calcium carbonate from the water and laid this hard mineral down around themselves. The result was a hard mat that built up to form a reef.

When cyanobacteria first evolved, animal life did not exist. But by Cambrian times these crustlike reefs attracted animals that needed a safe anchorage so that they could collect their food. Foremost among them were archaeocyathans—spongelike animals that grew into a wide variety of shapes, although few were more than 4 in. (10cm) high. Like the cyanobacteria,

archaeocyathans collected calcium carbonate from the water, and they used it to build up their meshlike skeletons. Many looked like small vases, with a central hollow, while others resembled mushrooms or a collection of branching twigs. Most of these animals lived on the surface of the reef, but some hid in crevices and cavities, sifting food that drifted down from above. As they grew upward in the light and warmth their dead remains became cemented together, steadily adding to the reef. Just like true sponges, archaeocyathans belonged to an unusual offshoot of the animal world. Instead of swallowing food through a mouth, as most animals do, they collected it by pumping water through tiny holes, or pores, in their bodies. As the water flowed through the pores anything edible was filtered out and digested.

Archaeocyathans grew in warm, tropical waters, but unlike true sponges, their reign was relatively short. A few species survived into the closing stages of the Cambrian Period, but at that point the entire group became extinct.

31

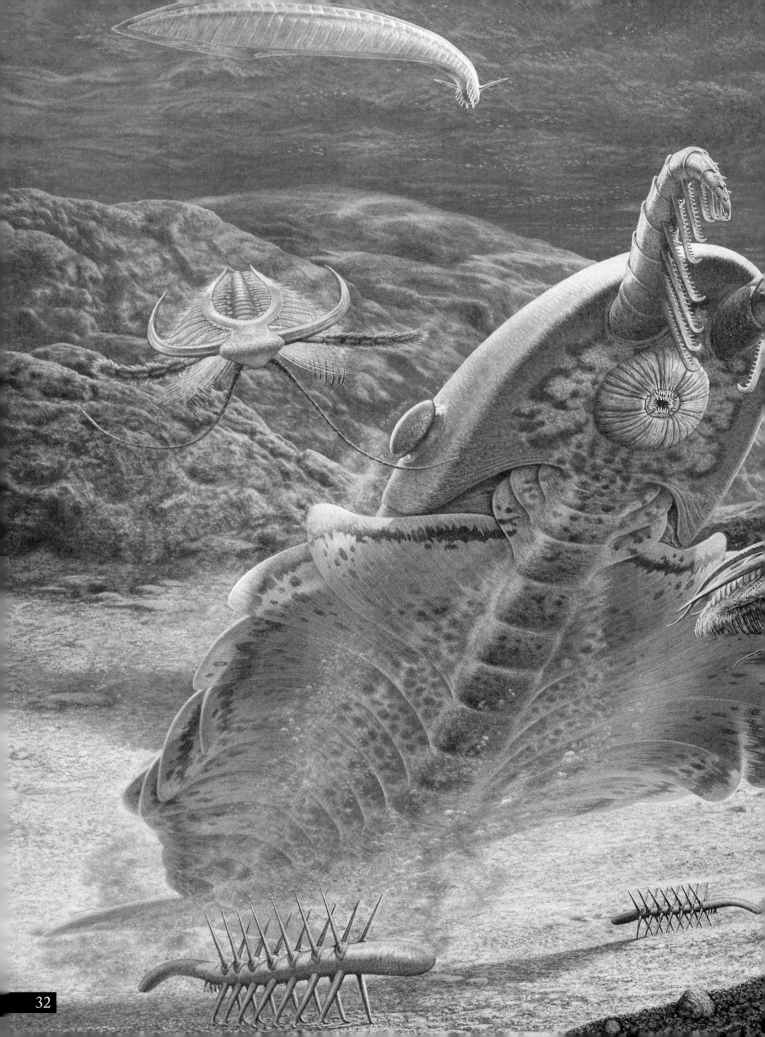

A SEABED GRAVEYARD

Rearing up over its prey, Anomalocaris—a giant shrimplike predator from the Cambrian Period—moves in to make a kill. Its intended victim, an animal called Marella, *speeds away by beating its slender legs. These two animals, like all the ones shown here, were found as fossils in the legendary Burgess Shale. (See key on page 34.)*

KEY TO PREVIOUS PAGES

1. PIKAIA
2. MARELLA
3. ANOMALOCARIS
4. STROMATOLITES
5. BRANCHING
   ARCHAEOCYATHAN
6. DINOMISCHUS
7. OTTOIA
8. HALLUCIGENIA

BURGESS SHALE

DISCOVERED IN 1909, IN CANADA'S ROCKY MOUNTAINS, THE BURGESS SHALE CONTAINS TENS OF THOUSANDS OF FOSSILS, MANY WELL PRESERVED. TOGETHER, THEY PAINT A VIVID PICTURE OF LIFE IN THE CAMBRIAN SEAS.

The Burgess Shale fossil formation was found by the American paleontologist Charles D. Walcott during a fossilhunt in northwest Canada. The animals in the shale lived on or near the seabed and were victims of underwater avalanches, which trapped them almost instantly in fine-grained mud. Because the mud was soft and contained very little oxygen, it preserved its victims remarkably well.

DOMINANT ARTHROPODS

The largest fossils in the Burgess Shale belong to arthropods—animals with a hard outer case that bends at flexible joints. Today the most common arthropods include insects, spiders, and crustaceans. In Cambrian times, these different groups did not exist yet. Instead, Cambrian arthropods included trilobites and some remarkable animals found in the Burgess Shale.

The top predator of the Burgess Shale was *Anomalocaris*, a name that means "unusual shrimp." The specimens in the Burgess Shale are up to 2 ft. (60cm) long. Ones found more recently, from Cambrian rocks in China, are over twice as large as this. *Anomalocaris* swam by rippling flaps along its sides, and it attacked its prey with a pair of fearsome mouthparts that looked like legs. Its mouth was disk-shaped and had a ring of teeth that it used to crush hard-bodied prey. Other predatory arthropods included *Sanctacaris*, which looked like a smaller version of *Anomalocaris* with a blunter head.

The most common Burgess Shale animal, called *Marella*, was another arthropod, but a much more delicate and graceful animal. It had long head spines sweeping back in elegant curves and two pairs of feelers or antennae. Rarely more than 0.8 in. (2cm) long, it had many pairs of legs and probably fed by picking up small animals or dead remains on the surface of the seabed.

The Burgess Shale also includes many trilobites—a group of arthropods whose bodies were divided lengthwise into three lobes. Trilobites went on to become some of the most successful invertebrates of the Paleozoic Era, and they were among the most important casualties during the mass extinction that brought it to a close.

SOFT-BODIED ANIMALS

The Burgess Shale also contains much rarer fossils, showing the complete outlines of soft-bodied animals. A typical example is *Ottoia*, a burrowing worm up to 6 in. (15cm) long. Its burrow was U-shaped, and it lurked inside it, feeling for prey on the surface with a spike-tipped proboscis that could be extended like a trunk. When the trunk made contact with anything edible, it was swallowed whole. Fossils of *Ottoia* contain food remains—including chunks of other *Ottoia* worms, suggesting that the animal was cannibalistic.

The shale includes fossils of *Pikaia*, a soft-bodied animal with a reinforcing rod running down its body. This feature means that it was probably an early chordate—the group to which vertebrates also belong.

MYSTERY ANIMALS

Some Burgess Shale animals have no modern equivalent, leaving scientists guessing about how they were related to the rest of the animal world. Animals such as *Hallucigenia*, *Opabinia*, and *Wiwaxia* now seem bizarre. The original fossils of *Hallucigenia* showed what seemed to be two rows of spiny legs and a set of short tentacles emerging from the back. These were all attached to a short, wormlike body without an obvious head. Working from these remains, *Hallucigenia* was reconstructed with the animal walking on its spines and its tentacles waving above it. However, since then further fossils have shown that researchers had mistakenly put the animal upside down. There are actually two sets of tentacles, and it is these that are *Hallucigenia*'s legs.

Opabinia looked like a shrimp, but had a bizarre claw-tipped snout, and *Wiwaxia* was like an armored cushion that cruised across the seabed. Their ancestry remains a mystery, hidden in undiscovered fossils.

◁ *With its eccentric snout,* Opabinia *captures* Amwiskia. Opabinia *had five eyes, a body divided into segments, and rows of swimming flaps.* Amwiskia *had a flattened body and a horizontal tail.*

△ *When* Anomalocaris *died its body often broke up. For many years, its mouth disks were thought to be the remains of a jellyfish and its forelimbs parts of a shrimp. Their true identity was established in 1985.*

◁ Sanctacaris *used its crushing mouthparts to attack animals on the seabed. Here one pursues an animal called* Leanchoilia *(far left), while behind it, another attacks a* Wiwaxia.

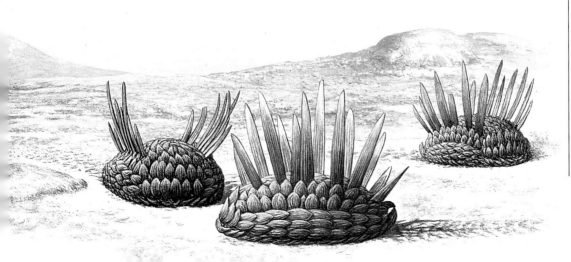

ORDOVICIAN PERIOD

WHEN THE ORDOVICIAN PERIOD STARTED, 505 MILLION YEARS AGO, ANIMAL LIFE WAS FOUND ONLY IN THE SEA. BY THE TIME IT ENDED, ANIMALS HAD TAKEN THEIR FIRST TENTATIVE STEPS ONTO LAND.

During the Ordovician Period almost all the world's land was south of the equator. Africa lay over the South Pole, joined to South America, Antarctica, and Australia, and together these land masses made up a giant continent called Gondwana. Ordovician animals thrived in the shallow seas, but climate change eventually brought these good times to a close. Ancient scratch marks created by glaciers show that a large ice cap developed over Gondwana and, at the close of the Ordovician Period, conditions became so cold that over half of the world's animal species became extinct.

▷ *Nautiloids were the largest animals in the Ordovician seas. Forms with straight and coiled shells, like the ones shown here, hunted over an underwater landscape carpeted with algae, corals, and crinoids—distant relatives of starfish. Drifting or planktonic animals were common, but most animals still fed on or near the seabed. Here, a snaillike mollusk crawls across the reef in the foreground, flanked by brachiopods that are filtering their food from the water.*

FILLING THE GAP

Like all major chapters in Earth's history, the Ordovician started with animals recovering from a round of extinctions. Compared to the mass extinction that ended the Ordovician, these were small, but they particularly affected the trilobites, which had become the most important arthropods of the time. So the Ordovician Period opened with a large number of biological vacancies —ones that evolution soon started to fill.

One group of animals that moved into this gap were the nautiloids—mollusks related to today's pearly nautiluses and more distantly to octopuses and squids. Unlike earlier mollusks, which lived on the seabed, nautiloids were able to swim. They could hover motionless above the seabed, watching for prey with well-developed eyes, or dart quickly through the sea by squirting a jet of water backward from their body cavity.

This new way of life was made possible by the unusual design of nautiloid shells. They were conical, or coiled, but instead of having a single internal chamber, like a snail's shell, they had a whole series of them, separated by thin partitions. The animal's body filled only the largest and most recent chamber, and the chambers behind it were hollow and filled with gas. A nautiloid could control the amount of gas in the chambers, allowing it to rise and fall like a submarine.

This new shell design was a sign of the times. Instead of hugging the seabed, more and more animals were starting to venture into the open water above.

VACUUM-CLEANER FISH

Although fishlike animals have been found from the Cambrian Period, the Ordovician is the point when they become widespread as fossils. Compared to nautiloids, these early vertebrates were small animals, and their downward-pointing mouths suggest that they fed on the seabed. They did not have jaws, although they probably could have moved their lips. At first most of them were like living vacuum cleaners, sucking up sediment and particles of food.

These fish—known as heterostracans— relied for survival on a bony shield that covered the front of their bodies. This reinforced plating became a common feature in early vertebrates, and it marked the start of an underwater arms race that was to continue for hundreds of millions of years.

REFUGE ON LAND

As the seas became more populated and more dangerous some animals sought refuge in fresh water and in the marshy shallows along the shore. Food grew here, in the form of simple matlike plants, but air quickly dries out living cells, so for most soft-bodied animals, emerging from damp mud and onto dry land would have been hazardous. Arthropods already had allover body cases that would have helped stop them from drying out. There are no direct remains of these pioneering animals, but tracks in fossilized mud show that they were probably the first to emerge on land, 450 million years ago.

THE AGE OF ANCIENT LIFE

ORDOVICIAN ANIMALS

The Ordovician Period was a time when invertebrates were still the unchallenged rulers of the ocean floor. Like today's invertebrates, some were able to move around, but many others lived alone or in groups, anchored to the seabed. These anchored animals gathered food that drifted within reach. They did not need eyes or large brains. But for moving animals, life was more demanding and more dangerous. They relied on sharp senses to find food, and quick reactions to avoid being attacked by other predators.

△ *Arandaspis was a heterostracan, or armored, jawless fish. Like other early fish, it swam by flicking its tail, and did not have any fins.*

△ *Discovered in South Africa in the early 1990s, Promissum was a giant conodont measuring 15.7 in. (40cm) in length. Its bulbous eyes suggest that it was an active hunter.*

▽ *Early horseshoe crabs crawled across the seabed on five pairs of legs. Today there are four species of these living fossils on the east coasts of North America and Asia.*

ARMORED ARTHROPODS

When arthropods first appeared, in Early Cambrian times, their bodies were small, and their body cases, or exoskeletons, were paper-thin. But by the beginning of the Ordovician several lines of arthropods had evolved their body cases into suits of armor to protect themselves from attack. One group of armored arthropods common in Ordovician times was the horseshoe crabs.

Despite their name, these animals were not true crabs, but members of a line that later produced spiders and scorpions. The front of their body was protected by a domed shield, or carapace, which completely hid their mouth and legs. The back of the body was protected by a second, smaller shield and ended in a long, spiny tail. This unusual design is clearly shown by fossils, but there is a much easier way of seeing how the horseshoe crab's body worked, because these animals still survive today. They are not the same species that lived in Ordovician times, but amazingly they have changed very little in over 400 million years.

Ordovician horseshoe crabs fed on small seabed animals using pincer-tipped legs to pick up their food. Their pincers were hidden away underneath their head shields, which limited their size. Some close relatives of horseshoe crabs—eurypterids, or sea scorpions—carried their pincers out in the open. In the Ordovician Period most sea scorpions were relatively small, but during the Silurian Period, which followed, they became the largest arthropods of the time.

MYSTERIOUS CONODONTS

For over a century scientists collected and cataloged huge numbers of tiny, toothlike fossils that date back to the Ordovician and sometimes beyond. Known as conodonts (because they are often cone-shaped), these

ORDOVICIAN ANIMALS

△ *This view of an Ordovician reef is based on Newfoundland fossils almost 500 million years old. Two nautiloids scan the seabed, while trilobites and gastropods (snaillike mollusks) creep over the surface below them. Clusters of crinoids, bent over by the current, filter out small particles of food.*

1. **STRAIGHT-SHELLED NAUTILOID**
2. **COILED NAUTILOID**
3. **TRILOBITE**
4. **GASTROPOD**
5. **CORAL**
6. **CRINOID**

objects clearly belonged to animals because their shapes evolved as time went by. These shapes are so characteristic that geologists could often estimate the age of rocks simply by looking at the conodonts that they contain. Despite years of searching, the animals that grew these miniature teeth were never found.

A breakthrough came in 1993 when fossils were discovered in Scotland of complete conodont animals with their teeth. Further fossils have been found in North America and South Africa, including one species, *Promissum*, which dates back to Ordovician times. The mystery animals turned out to be creatures with slender, snakelike bodies and well-developed eyes. Some fossils show traces of V-shaped muscle blocks and a notochord—features that are found in vertebrates and their relatives.

Many scientists think that conodonts were vertebrates, which would make them some of the earliest to have evolved. But, unlike the

main vertebrate line that went on to produce four-legged animals, the conodonts did not last. By the end of the Triassic, when the first dinosaurs appeared, conodont teeth vanish from the fossil record, showing that this group of animals had become extinct.

PLANT LOOK-ALIKES

During the Ordovician a rare event occurred: a completely new group of animals appeared —one of the very few to appear after the Cambrian explosion (page 28). Known as bryozoans, these were tiny invertebrates protected by boxlike skeletons. They grew side by side in colonies, forming shapes that often looked like plants. Bryozoans proved to be a very successful addition to the animal world and are still widespread today.

The Ordovician seabed was also home to a collection of much larger plantlike animals, the crinoids, or sea lilies. Belonging to the same group of animals as starfish and sea urchins, they had a long stalk made of chalky disks and a crown of brittle arms that gathered food. Later some crinoids broke free from this static existence and took up a free-ranging life in the sea. Both kinds of crinoids still exist today.

THE SILURIAN PERIOD

DURING THE SILURIAN PERIOD, AS THE EARTH'S CLIMATE BECAME WARMER AND MORE STABLE, ANIMAL LIFE RECOVERED IN THE SEAS. AT THE SAME TIME, ANIMALS MANAGED TO STRENGTHEN THEIR HOLD ON LAND.

When the Silurian Period started, 438 million years ago, animal life was emerging from the worst catastrophe so far. During the Silurian conditions improved: the climate warmed, and sea levels rose, creating shallow seas that triggered a surge in animal evolution. On land important changes were also underway. The first true plants appeared, creating ankle-high jungles that grew on marshy ground. By the time the Silurian ended, after only 30 million years, land-based animals were widespread, although few were more than an inch long.

▷ *Crawling over the seabed, a giant eurypterid—sea scorpion—catches a meal. These huge arthropods probably lived by hunting and scavenging. Like most modern arthropods, their eyes were compound—consisting of many compartments. Eurypterids would probably have been poor at registering detail, but very good at spotting movement.*

ARMORED PREDATORS

In Silurian times the largest sea animals were giant eurypterids, or sea scorpions— relatives of horseshoe crabs (page 38). One species, called *Pterygotus rhenanius*, was nearly 10 ft. (3m) long, making it a deadly threat to other animals as it roamed the seabed. Like other eurypterids, it had an armor-plated body that could bend at flexible joints. Four pairs of its legs were used for walking; the fifth pair—at the rear —was flattened and worked like oars. Slung underneath its head was a pair of powerful pincers; the head itself was equipped with a pair of saucer-sized eyes. As the sea scorpion lumbered over the seabed, animals would have panicked, but their escape would have been cut short by a lunge of its claws.

Eurypterids lived in brackish water as well as the sea. The Silurian Period marked the heyday of eurypterids as the top predators in water. But fish were also increasing in size. Eventually fish would become a threat to the eurypterids, but during the Silurian things were the other way around.

WEIGHTY MATTERS

While sea scorpions hunted in the shallows other arthropods were evolving on land. These included primitive centipedes and arachnids, the ancestors of spiders and their relatives. These land-based arthropods went on to become extremely successful, but none of them ever rivaled eurypterids in size. Without water to buoy it up, a giant armor-plated body is so heavy that it is almost impossible to move. This factor explains why today's land-based arthropods, such as insects and spiders, are still relatively small, but aquatic species, such as lobsters, can grow to a much larger size.

LIFE AFLOAT

At the other extreme in size, the Silurian seas teemed with planktonic animals, ones that were small and light enough to drift in open water. These included the developing young, or larvae, of mollusks and trilobites and also a group of remarkable invertebrates called graptolites. Graptolites appeared in the Cambrian and flourished for 200 million years. Then the entire group became extinct.

Individual graptolites were rarely more than a few millimeters long, but they lived in colonies or groups that could be 8 in. (20cm) or more in length. Each member of the colony produced a hard, protective cup, built out of a material similar to the one found in mammals' hooves and claws, and the cups were joined together to form a colony. The shape of the colonies varied enormously. Some looked like leaves or small bunches of twigs; others resembled tuning forks, wheels, or even spiders' webs.

Fossil graptolites are extremely common, but scientists once had difficulty deciding what they were. Some were thought to be fossilized plants or even naturally occurring crystals that had grown through sedimentary rock. It is now thought that graptolites were hemichordates—distant relatives of obscure wormlike animals that still exist today.

THE AGE OF ANCIENT LIFE

SILURIAN ANIMALS

Despite the lead taken by small arthropods, the vast majority of Silurian animals lived in freshwater or in the sea. Underwater life was still dominated by animals without backbones, but among vertebrates, some momentous changes were under way. One of these was the evolution of the first fish with true jaws. In time jaws turned out to be a decisive trait, allowing vertebrates to become the most widespread large animals on Earth. But during the Silurian that still lay in the future, as jawed and jawless fishes experimented with different ways of life.

▷ Jamoytius *belonged to a group of fish called anaspids, which had over a dozen gill openings arranged like portholes in the side of a ship. It was about 1 ft. (30cm) long and had three long fins—one on its back and two on its sides as well as a fin on its tail.*

▽ *For early fish, sea scorpions like this* Pterygotus *were a major hazard. But as fish evolved many of them became faster and more maneuverable, moving away from the seabed and the dangers that it held.*

JAWED FISH

When the Silurian Period opened, the only fish in existence were ones that did not have jaws. To us a jawless mouth may sound like a contradiction in terms, but the numerous fossils of jawless fish suggest that it worked adequately. However, jawless fish had limited options when it came to taking in food. One feeding method was to use the mouth like a scoop to dig up sediment—a technique that was probably used by *Jamoytius*, a common species of the time. Alternatively, the mouth could be used like a sucker, attaching the fish to its food. This feeding method is used by lampreys—parasitic animals that are among the few jawless fish that still survive today.

In the early Silurian a group of fish called acanthodians, or spiny sharks, developed a radical alternative to both these ways of feeding. A part of their skeleton—the struts that supported its first pair of gills—gradually turned into a set of jaws. Unlike fish with jawless mouths, these fish could use their jaws as weapons to attack their prey. They could also bite off pieces of food, instead of having to swallow prey whole.

THE ACANTHODIANS

Despite their name, spiny sharks were not true sharks, because these did not evolve until Devonian times. However, they did have bony spines that supported their fins. One common late Silurian, called *Climatius*, was about the size of a typical goldfish, but some later forms grew to over 6.6 ft. (2m) long. Their skeletons were made of cartilage rather than bone, and they had strongly upturned tails. Unlike true sharks, acanthodians had large eyes and short snouts, suggesting that smell played little part in finding prey. Their teeth were small, and although they were constantly replaced, they often grew only in the lower jaw. But they did have another first—a flap, called an operculum, that covered their gills. This could be used like a pump, allowing these fish to breathe without having to swim. For a while spiny sharks were the world's only vertebrates that had jaws, but this unique status was not to last. Once the Silurian came to an end, new groups of jawed fish appeared, and by the early stages of the Permian Period these original trailblazers became extinct.

CORAL REEFS

Until Silurian times algae and sponges had been common inhabitants of reefs, but corals were rarer animals. During the Silurian things changed: corals became widespread, and the first coral reefs began to form. The corals that we know today had not evolved yet, but Silurian corals were like them in many ways. Some species were solitary, meaning that individuals lived on their own, but the reef-building species formed large colonies, with hard cases or cups firmly cemented together. As young coral colonies developed, the older ones beneath them

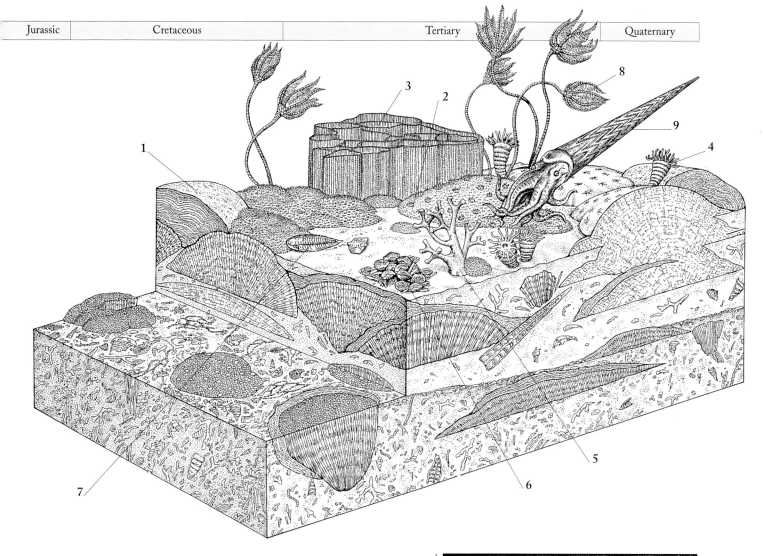

△ *This view of a Silurian reef is based on fossils that are about 430 million years old. Found in England, it contains tabulate and rugose corals—two groups that became extinct at the end of the Paleozoic Era. Silurian reefs gave safe anchorage for other invertebrates, such as brachiopods, bryozoans, and crinoids.*

died, forming layers of hard remains. These became glued together by dissolved minerals, turning them into deposits of solid rock.

The way that colonies grew gave each kind a distinctive shape. Some had branches that divided repeatedly, making them look like a set of antlers. These branching colonies often grew quickly but, because they were brittle, could only survive where there was no danger of being broken up by the waves. Others grew more slowly and had rounded or flattened shapes. These types were much better at surviving in rough water, and they often grew on the outer edges of reefs, where breakers rolled in from the open sea.

Modern reef-building corals generally need light to thrive, because they contain microscopic algae that live as onboard partners, using sunlight to make food. Early corals, on the other hand, survived entirely by catching tiny animals, which they trapped with tentacles that carried stinging cells. It was a highly effective system and can still be seen in corals and jellyfish today.

△ *Crinoids became increasingly successful during the Paleozoic. Their chalky stalks usually fell apart after they died, but the main part of the body, with its feeding arms, was often preserved in fossils (above).*

THE DEVONIAN PERIOD

OFTEN KNOWN AS THE AGE OF FISHES, THE DEVONIAN PERIOD WAS A TIME WHEN ANIMALS WITH BACKBONES BEGAN THEIR DOMINANCE OF LIFE IN THE SEA AND MADE THEIR FIRST MOVES ONTO LAND.

The Devonian Period began about 408 million years ago, at a time when major changes were taking place in the way the world looked. The giant continent of Gondwana still lay near the South Pole, but it was moving northward; and parts of Europe and North America, together with Greenland, were joined to form a single continent that straddled the equator. The climate was warm, and on land the simple, low-growing plants of Silurian times gradually gave way to ones that were much better at surviving out of water. By the time the Devonian ended the first forests had formed.

▷ The giant placoderm Dunkleosteus *closes in on a young* Cladoselache, *a species of primitive shark.* Dunkleosteus *had a set of tooth plates that lasted for life, while* Cladoselache, *like today's sharks, had dozens of triangular teeth that grew from the inside edge of its jaw, on a nonstop production line. Both of these early fish swam by waving their tails; their other fins were stiff and acted as stabilizers to keep them on course.*

JAWS REVISITED

Evolution has often invented the same adaptation in animal life several times. This is what seems to have happened during the Devonian Period with a group of fish called the placoderms. Placoderms had powerful jaws—bladelike plates that made effective teeth. But since placoderms were not direct descendants of the first jawed fish (page 42), most experts think that they must have evolved jaws themselves. As well as jaws these fish had two hard shields—one that covered the head and one on the front part of the trunk. The shields were connected by a pair of hinges, allowing the front of the head to lift when the fish bit into its prey.

Some placoderms lived on the seabed, where they fed on mollusks and other hard-bodied animals, but toward the Late Devonian others became hunters that lived in open water. Here they became some of the largest predators in the history of animal life so far. One of them, called *Dunkleosteus*, was nearly 13 ft. (4m) long, with mouth plates that could slice other fish in two.

FISH BRANCH OUT

During the Devonian placoderms shared the seas with several other groups of fish. They included jawless species with bizarrely shaped armored bodies (page 46), as well as nonarmored fish, which looked much more like the fish we know today. These nonarmored species were of two kinds: some had skeletons made of cartilage; others had ones made of bone.

The cartilaginous fish were the ancestors of today's sharks and rays. Their bodies were covered in small, rough scales known as denticles, and in their mouths specially enlarged denticles formed a never-ending supply of sharp teeth. Even from their early days many of these fish had the familiar sharklike shape, and by the Late Devonian one species, called *Cladoselache*, was already 6.6 ft. (2m) long. The bony fish were generally small and were covered in scales that became thinner and lighter as time passed. These fish developed gas-filled swim bladders that controlled their buoyancy and mobile fins that made them highly maneuverable.

One group of bony fish, called the lobe-fins, had fins with a fleshy base containing muscle and bone. These interest scientists greatly because they were the animals from which four-legged vertebrates evolved. Not all lobe-fins left the water: several species, including the lungfishes and the coelacanths, still live in freshwater or the sea to this day.

LIFE ON LAND

Despite many years of research, experts do not yet know which of the lobe-finned fish gave rise to primitive amphibians—the first vertebrates to live partly on land. But by the time the Devonian ended, the transition had been made. When the first amphibians appeared they would have seemed slow and awkward compared to other land creatures, but it was a move that would change the whole course of animal life.

THE AGE OF ANCIENT LIFE

DEVONIAN ANIMALS

During the Devonian invertebrate life continued to evolve, although not at the hectic pace that marked the Silurian. Spiral-shelled ammonoids developed from nautiloids, creating a group of mollusks often well preserved as fossils. Trilobites and sea scorpions were on the wane, although when the Devonian ended, both groups still managed to survive for a further 100 million years. But for animal life as a whole the key developments during the Silurian occurred among vertebrates—particularly those that pioneered the difficult move onto land.

▽ *This trio of jawless fish from Devonian times shows different forms of armor protection.* Drepanaspis *(top) and* Cephalaspis *(left) were both bottom-dwellers, with flattened undersides and tails that were triangular in cross section.* Pteraspis *(right) was more streamlined and was built for life in open water.*

FISH THAT WALKED
One of the striking features of the Devonian Period is the number of fish that had heavily armored heads. Armored fish are rare today, but during the Devonian a wide variety of them lived on the seabed and in rivers and lakes. Most of them were bottom-dwellers because their armor—while useful against predators—made swimming in open water hard work.

Among the placoderms (page 44) species that are common as fossils include *Bothriolepis*, which had a semicircular head shield and narrow pectoral (front) fins.

It may have used the fins for balancing on the bottom or perhaps for walking along riverbeds. Another species, called *Pterichthyodes*, looked like a fish that had swum into a bony box, leaving only its tail outside. It, too, had elongated pectoral fins, which may have allowed it to crawl across the mud in lakes. *Groenlandaspis*, a finger-sized species that lived in freshwater, was extremely widespread. Fossils of this little fish have been found not only in Greenland, but also as far away as Australia and Antarctica.

THE END OF ARMOR
Jawless fish also specialized in armor protection in Devonian times. One group, known as the osteostracans, are known for their flattened and horseshoe-shaped heads, which can be well preserved in fossils. One typical species, a freshwater fish called *Cephalaspis*, had a head shield that ended in two backward-pointing horns. The head shield was made of a single piece of bone, which meant that it probably could not grow once it had been fully formed. As a result the shield probably developed when the fish reached adult size. Like its relatives, *Cephalaspis* had another unusual feature—patches of sensory nerves on the sides and top of the shield. These probably helped it navigate or find food, perhaps by sensing vibrations or weak electrical fields.

Armored jawless fish also included species such as *Drepanaspis*, with a shield that was almost round, and *Pteraspis*, an open-water species that had a sharply pointed snout. For tens of millions of years these armored animals were very successful, but as other fish began to evolve alongside them, speed and maneuverability eventually proved to be more useful in the struggle for survival.

LUNGS AND LIMBS
In Early Devonian times tropical lakes and rivers became the home of the world's first lungfish—fish that had gills,

THE FIRST AMPHIBIANS

While Devonian fish left many fossils, Devonian amphibians are extremely rare. Fossils of the two best-known examples—*Ichthyostega* and *Acanthostega*—were both found in Greenland. They had long, fishlike bodies and four legs, but webbed, fishlike tails. Despite their fishy origins, these animals had many adaptations for life on land. They breathed partly through lungs and partly through their skin, and their skeletons were strengthened to support the extra weight they had to bear out of water. Reconstructions of *Ichthyostega* and *Acanthostega* often show these two animals hunting on land, with their bodies half-crawling and half-slithering across marshy Devonian landscapes. But recent studies of their fossils show that their legs may have had difficulty supporting their weight, making some scientists doubt if they were as agile on land as was once assumed. Instead of being land animals that sometimes took to the water, the real situation may have been the other way around. For *Ichthyostega* and *Acanthostega* water would have been a place to feed and breed, and land would have made a useful refuge from the predatory fish that shared their freshwater home.

◁ With a body up to 2 ft. (60cm) long, including its webbed tail, Acanthostega had webbed feet with eight fingers and toes. Apart from this, it looked much like a giant version of today's salamanders. However, it had many fishlike features, including a streamlined head and a system of sensors called a lateral line, which today's fish use to detect waterborne vibrations.

▽ Grasping a centipede firmly between its jaws, Icthyostega prepares to swallow its prey. In theory, at 3.3 ft. (1m) long it would have been able to tackle many land animals of its time. However, whether it could actually hunt like this is a matter of debate—some experts think it made slow progress out of water.

but could also breathe air when the water's oxygen supply was low. This was particularly useful in warm, stagnant water, where other fish ran the risk of suffocation. One of the earliest of lungfish, called *Dipterus*, is known from fossils discovered in Europe and North America. It was about 19.7 in. (50cm) long, with a cylindrical body and sharply upturned tail.

FINS AND LIMBS

Lungfish belonged to the group known as the lobe-fins (page 44), which had bone and muscle in their fins, making them similar to limbs. This combination of lungs and limblike fins made some biologists believe that they were the ancestors of amphibians, and therefore of all four-legged vertebrates. But a closer look at lungfish shows that they probably did not make the move onto land. Today a different group of lobe-fins are thought to be the most likely candidates for this position in the vertebrate family tree. Known as rhipidistians, they included species such as *Eusthenopteron*, a blunt-headed fish 4 ft. (1.2m) long, with fin bones arranged like those in an amphibian's legs. *Eusthenopteron* also had a braincase like the ones found in early amphibians, providing further evidence that it, or one of its relatives, produced animals that made the move onto land.

THE CARBONIFEROUS PERIOD

A TIME OF IMPORTANT DEVELOPMENTS FOR LIFE ON LAND, THE CARBONIFEROUS SAW THE GROWTH OF VAST LOWLAND FORESTS AND THE EVOLUTION OF THE FIRST REPTILES AND OF THE FIRST ANIMALS THAT COULD FLY.

The Carboniferous Period began 360 million years ago, after a mass extinction (thought to have been triggered by a cooling climate) that killed up to 70 percent of marine animals. In the Western Hemisphere land stretched almost from pole to pole, while in the east most of the world was covered by a Pacific-sized ocean. During the Carboniferous rising sea levels, together with a generally warm and humid climate, created perfect conditions for forests of giant club mosses and ferns, growing on swampy, low-lying ground. The remains of these forests eventually turned into seams of coal, giving the Carboniferous its name.

▷ Hylonomus, *one of the world's earliest known reptiles, was about 8 in. (20cm) long. It was fully at home on land. Its remains were discovered inside fossilized tree stumps, together with those of other Carboniferous animals. It seems likely that* Hylonomus *fell into the tree stumps while hunting and was unable to get out.*

ADAPTING TO LIFE ON LAND

At the beginning of the Carboniferous early amphibians were still tied to a water-based way of life. Like today's frogs and toads, they laid their eggs in ponds and streams, and their young went through an aquatic tadpole stage, initially breathing through feathery gills. Even as adults they had to stay close to water, because their skins were thin and they had to stay moist.

In the Carboniferous extensive swamps meant that animals like these were rarely short of somewhere to breed. But water-based life had its dangers. Fish ate a large proportion of amphibian tadpoles, as well as the adults themselves. Amphibians also faced great competition for food—not only from fish and water scorpions, but also from each other. These were just some of the reasons why nature favored amphibians that were better at coping with life on dry land.

BECOMING WATERPROOF

For water-based animals with thin skins the greatest danger on land was drying out. The problem began to diminish when some amphibians developed thicker skin that was protected by scales. This kind of skin acted like a waterproof jacket, keeping most of the body's moisture inside. More importantly, they evolved a new kind of egg—one that was surrounded by a tough membrane called an amnion, which was itself enclosed in a porous shell. The membrane and shell let oxygen in so that the developing embryo could breathe, but they let very little water escape into the air outside. This amniotic egg was an immense leap forward, because it allowed vertebrates to breed away from water. Instead of hatching into swimming tadpoles, their young hatched out as miniature versions of their parents, fully equipped for life on land.

FROM AMPHIBIAN TO REPTILE

In the hunt for the first reptiles, scientists have examined a wide range of fossils to find the earliest ones that fall on the reptile side of the amphibian-reptile divide. Skin and eggs are often missing from the fossil record, but another sign of reptile status is a rib cage that can expand. Unlike amphibians, which gulp air when they breathe, reptiles use their rib cage to suck air into their lungs.

At present the earliest animals that seem to meet all these criteria are *Palaeothyris* and *Hylonomus*, two lizardlike creatures that have been found in present-day Nova Scotia. They were slim and agile and had well-developed legs without any webbing on their feet and a cylindrical, rather than a flattened, tail. *Palaeothyris* and *Hylonomus* lived in the swampy surroundings of Carboniferous forests, but as reptiles evolved they moved farther and farther away from damp surroundings. Eventually—well before the age of the dinosaurs—they would spread to the driest places on Earth.

THE AGE OF ANCIENT LIFE

CARBONIFEROUS ANIMALS

On land invertebrates still made up the vast majority of animal species during the Carboniferous, but their place was no longer secure. Four-legged vertebrates, or tetrapods, were evolving fast, and by the Late Carboniferous they became the largest predators of their day. Meanwhile, in the freshwater and the seas there was growing success for the cartilaginous and bony fish, mirrored by a steady decline in fish without jaws. During this period in the earth's history crinoids, or sea lilies, continued to thrive, and in some places they formed great underwater forests that carpeted the ocean floor.

△ With its webbed tail and small, widely spaced legs, Eogyrinus was well equipped for hunting in shallow water, but not suited to life on land. Other amphibians of the Carboniferous—particularly the smaller species—spent much of their adult life out of water, just as most amphibians do today.

EARLY TETRAPODS
In the Carboniferous many of the largest hunters lived like today's crocodiles and alligators, attacking their prey in lakes and shallows, but sometimes dragging themselves up on dry land. One of the largest was *Eogyrinus*, over 13 ft. (4m) from the end of its snout to the tip of its webbed tail. *Eogyrinus* was an amphibian, and it belonged to a group called the anthracosaurs—a name that means "'coal lizards"—which survived until the Permian Period and then became extinct. Anthracosaurs are thought to be the group from which the reptiles evolved.

Another anthracosaur, *Seymouria*, was better adapted to life on land, with stronger legs than *Eogyrinus* and no webbing on its tail. Although it looked like a reptile as an adult, fossils of its young show signs of a lateral line—the sensory system used during their life in water. Because it grew up in the water, *Seymouria* fails the reptile test.

AMPHIBIAN ARRAY
Several different groups, all now extinct, shared the Carboniferous lakes and swamps with their anthracosaur relatives. Among them were amphibians called temnospondyls, a group of species that are the probable ancestors of frogs and toads. One of the largest was an animal called *Eryops*, which looked like a small, frog-eyed crocodile supported by stubby legs. *Eryops* was about 6.6 ft. (2m) long and, like all amphibians, had thin, scaleless skin. It also had bony plates along its back, which may have protected it when it hauled itself out of the shallows. Although *Eryops* was large, it was not the biggest of its group. One species, called *Mastodonsaurus*, had a skull over 3.3 ft. (1m) long—large enough to make it a threat to many of the other amphibians around it.

Over the years paleontologists have found many fossilized tadpoles of *Eryops* and its relatives. Today they are recognized for what they are, but earlier they were thought to be separate species.

REPTILES AND THEIR SKULLS
The earliest reptiles evolved in the Late Carboniferous, and included *Palaeothyris* and *Hylonomus* (page 48). Despite their place at the foot of the reptile family tree, these two animals look like lizards and could be mistaken for them if they lived today. However, internally they had several features that made them distinct. One of the most important was that their skulls had no openings apart from the ones that housed their nostrils and eyes. Reptiles that are built in this way are called anapsids, which literally means "without arches." Anapsids inherited this kind of skull from their amphibian ancestors, and only turtles and tortoises have this kind of skull today. Other reptiles went on to develop extra openings; these reduced weight and provided anchorage for their jaw muscles. Synapsids evolved one pair of extra openings, positioned behind the eyes,

CARBONIFEROUS ANIMALS

▽ Meganeuropsis was a giant dragonfly that flew over swamps. Like modern dragonflies, its two pairs of wings could beat in opposite directions, allowing it to hover like a helicopter as it watched for prey.

while diapsids evolved two. These fossae, or hollows, are of interest because they help in piecing together the path of evolution. Synapsids include animals that went on to produce mammals; diapsids include the ruling reptiles or archosaurs—the group to which all dinosaurs belonged.

TAKING TO THE AIR

For anyone averse to bugs and insects, the Carboniferous landscape would have been a nightmare. Scorpions up to 29.5 in (75cm) long crawled over the ground in search of prey, and giant cockroaches and millipedes vied for rotting plant remains. Centipedes preyed with poison fangs on other land animals after dark. Primitive dragonflies swooped on airborne insects over pools and among trees, flying on wings that could be over 2 ft. (60cm) from tip to tip. Insects were the first animals to fly, and in Carboniferous times they had the air to themselves. However, scientists have found few clues to how and

when the first winged species evolved. According to one theory insect wings may have developed from the flattened pads that some fossil species have attached to their body segments. Initially these pads may have been used for temperature regulation or perhaps in courtship displays, but if they became large enough, they could have been used for gliding. To become true wings they would have then had to develop hinges at the point where they meet the body. Their owners would have had to develop flight muscles by modifying existing muscles inside the middle part of the body, or thorax. As this happened they would have changed from gliders to the first true aviators.

Because winged insects were well developed by the Carboniferous Period, it is likely that they first appeared in the Devonian, but fossils have yet to be discovered that date this far back in time.

▽ Terrestrial scorpions evolved from ancestors that lived in water. Aquatic scorpions breathed through gills, but land-dwelling forms developed book lungs inside their bodies. In a book lung air flows past thin flaps that are stacked like pages of a book.

51

THE PERMIAN PERIOD

THE PERMIAN PERIOD WAS THE FINAL STAGE
IN THE PALEOZOIC ERA. IT IS KNOWN CHIEFLY
FOR THE DRAMATIC WAY THAT IT ENDED—
WITH THE LARGEST MASS EXTINCTION IN
THE HISTORY OF LIFE ON EARTH.

By the beginning of the Permian, 286 million years ago, the earth's land masses had converged to form a single supercontinent called Pangaea. Because Pangaea was so vast, climatic conditions on land varied enormously. Over the South Pole an ice cap remained from Carboniferous times, but across the tropics and much of the north, Pangaea was a place of baking heat and little rain. In these arid conditions the moisture-loving trees of Carboniferous times went into retreat, to be replaced by conifers and other seed-forming plants that were better at coping with drought.

*▷ Basking in the early morning sunshine, pelycosaurs soak up warmth through their vertical sails. Both the species shown here—*Dimetrodon *(foreground) and* Edaphosaurus *(background)—lived in the early Permian, and grew to a length of about 10 ft. (3m).* Dimetrodon *was a predator, armed with stabbing teeth.* Edaphosaurus *was a herbivore. Their sails were kept permanently upright by struts of bone.*

WATER AND WARMTH

Evolution cannot plan ahead, so it could not prepare animals for the changed conditions of Permian times. But reptiles turned out to be ideally suited to the drier climate that developed when the Permian began. They spread across the supercontinent, to habitats where amphibians could not survive. As they evolved they became better at economizing with water until they could live in desert conditions, like many reptiles do today.

Reptiles also had to deal with the large temperature changes that often occur on land. In water and wetlands, where the first four-legged vertebrates evolved, temperature changes were gradual, and the highest were rarely very high. But in Pangaea's interior it could be close to freezing at dawn and over 104°F (40°C) by the middle of the day. Because reptiles were (and still are) ectothermic, or cold-blooded, their body temperatures rose and fell with the temperature of their surroundings. They would be almost immobilized by the cold at dawn, but by noon, they could be at risk of overheating.

AN INSIDE SOLUTION

Early reptiles would have dealt with this problem in the same way that reptiles do now: by basking in the sunshine when they were cold or by hiding in the shade when they were too hot. In time some reptiles—most notably the pelycosaurs—developed tall sails that probably acted as heat exchangers, helping them warm up and make an earlier start to the day. But later in the Permian descendants of the pelycosaurs called therapsids evolved a very different answer to the problem of temperature control. Instead of depending on the sun's warmth, they started to conserve the heat that their own bodies generated by breaking down food. In other words, they became endothermic, or warm-blooded. To keep in heat, they used something quite new—fur.

WARM-BLOODED VERTEBRATES

Fur rarely shows up in fossils, and there is no direct evidence that furred therapsids actually existed during the Permian Period, or at any later time. However, several pieces of evidence suggest that it is highly likely. One is that therapsids evolved adaptations that improved their breathing rate and oxygen supply—something that is essential in animals that burn lots of food. Another is that some therapsids lived in the south of Pangaea, where winter conditions would have been severe. This is an unlikely habitat for a cold-blooded reptile. But for one that could keep itself warm by burning food, life would have been much easier.

Therapsids were the animals that went on to give rise to the mammals, but they were not mammals themselves. Even though Permian forms probably had fur, they were unlike mammals as we know them today. But being warm-blooded was a key innovation—one that would eventually allow four-legged vertebrates to conquer every habitat of Earth, including high mountains and polar ice.

◁ *Cacops was an armored Permian amphibian. About 15.7 in. (40cm) long, it was well adapted to life on land, but probably laid its eggs in water.*

PERMIAN ANIMALS

During the Permian therapsids—or mammallike reptiles—became an increasingly important part of life on land. Although they never reached the gigantic sizes of reptiles in the Mesozoic Era, they were the dinosaurs of their day. Soon after they first appeared, they evolved into a variety of hunters and plant eaters, reaching sizes of up to 16.4 ft. (5m) long and weights of over 1 ton. In the Permian four-legged vertebrates also included a wide variety of amphibians, pelycosaurs, and the archosaurs, the group of animals to which the dinosaurs belonged.

▽ Anteosaurus *launches an attack on* Moschops *in a region of Gondwana that is now South Africa's Karoo Basin.*

THERAPSIDS OF THE KAROO
Much of our knowledge of Permian therapsids comes from fossils found in central and European Russia and in the Karoo, a region of South

Africa. The Karoo fossils often consist of complete skeletons, allowing animals to be reconstructed down to the smallest details.

One of the largest plant eaters from the Karoo was *Moschops*, an animal that grew to about 13 ft. (4m) in length. It had a much shorter tail than most of the earliest reptiles, and the typical barrel-shaped body of a large plant eater, supported by sturdy legs. *Moschops* also had a remarkably thick skull. Some paleontologists think that this would have been used in head-butting contests, although others have suggested that this bony growth might have been the result of disease. Despite its size, *Moschops* did not lead an entirely tranquil life, because the Karoo was home to some formidable flesh-eating therapsids, including *Anteosaurus*, which rivaled *Moschops* for size. In general build the two animals were similar, but *Moschops* had chisellike teeth, and *Anteosaurus* had extra-long stabbing teeth near the front of its jaws—the sign of an animal with a carnivorous way of life.

RUSSIAN THERAPSIDS
Russian therapsids included some decidedly strange-looking animals. One of the oddest was *Estemmenosuchus*, a name that means

◁ *While a herd of* Estemmenosuchus *wanders down to a lake to drink, a solitary* Eotitanosuchus *watches them from the opposite shore, sizing up the possibility of making a kill. In the generally dry conditions of Permian times oases like these would have made good hunting grounds.*

▽ *Watched by* Varanosaurus, *two* Caseas *lie on a sandy bank, soaking up the sunshine. Casea's sprawling gait meant that it rested with its body on the ground— unlike many plant eaters of later times, which spent most of their time on all fours.*

"crowned crocodile." With its bulky body and short tail, *Estemmenosuchus* bore very little resemblance to a crocodile, but it did have a crown of four hornlike outgrowths— two projecting from the sides of its face and two from the top of its head. These outgrowths could have been used for defense, but since they were short and blunt, a more likely explanation is that they were used to show an animal's status during courtship displays. The horns would have been largest in adult animals, particularly mature males.

Scientist disagree as to whether *Estemmenosuchus* was carnivorous, but another large therapsid from Late Permian Russia, called *Eotitanosuchus*, certainly was. It had saberlike canine teeth, set in a skull that had narrow and powerful jaws.

PERMIAN PELYCOSAURS

Although pelycosaurs gave rise to the therapsids, they continued to flourish alongside them during Permian times. The best-known examples are the sail-backed species (page 53), but the pelycosaur group also included animals that looked much more like some reptiles that exist today. One carnivorous species, called *Varanosaurus*, has been given its name because of its resemblance to today's monitor lizards and like them could be over 5 ft. (1.5m) long. Another species, called *Casea*, was a plant eater and a member of the last family of

pelycosaurs to appear. It had a fat, sprawling body like that of a modern iguana, with a small head and a slender tail. Its dentition was highly unusual, with peglike teeth in the upper jaw, but no teeth in its lower jaw—exactly the reverse of the arrangement in many large plant eaters today. This curious feature must have been an asset rather than a handicap, because *Casea*'s descendants became abundant and survived almost to the time when the Permian Period came to its calamitous close.

THE AGE OF ANCIENT LIFE

END OF AN ERA

About 245 million years ago the Permian Period came to an end in the greatest mass extinction since animal life began. Its effects were the worst in the oceans, where about 96 percent of all marine species died out; on land the figure was around 75 percent. The victims of this great calamity included trilobites, Paleozoic corals, and a number of other invertebrates, as well as the pelycosaurs, which in Permian times had been some of the most successful reptiles on land. By clearing away so many living species, this immense upheaval had a profound effect on the future course of animal evolution.

▷ *Some scientists believe that the existence of a single supercontinent, Pangaea, triggered environmental changes that devastated life at the end of the Permian.*

▷ *After existing for over 260 million years and surviving two mass extinctions, trilobites finally became extinct.*

▽ *Volcanic gases from eruptions may have trapped incoming heat and made temperatures spiral upward.*

MISSING EVIDENCE
Many theories have been put forward to explain the Permian mass extinction, but there are three or four primary explanations, or several of them acting together. The first of these—and the most quick-acting—is an impact by an asteroid or some other object from space. If this were large enough, it would have created a devastating shock wave that spread around the world, mirroring the event believed to have wiped out the dinosaurs (page 204). Chemical evidence has recently given weight to this idea, but scientists still think that the extinction was caused by natural changes on Earth.

A HOMEGROWN DISASTER
One leading Earth-centered theory is that a massive wave of volcanic eruptions blasted billions of tons of ash into the sky. If the eruptions continued over a long period, the ash clouds would have cut off much of the sunlight on which plant life depends. Without plants on land and microscopic algae in the sea, most animals would soon have perished. Signs of immense eruption have been found in Siberia.

Another possiblity is that falling sea levels in the Late Permian obliterated the shallow inshore waters on which much of marine life depended. As Pangaea had a relatively short coastline, this would have left corals and other invertebrates with a rapidly shrinking habitat. However, the decimation of land life is harder to explain, which is why falling sea levels may have been an additional factor in the mass extinction, rather than its main cause.

Many scientists think that the fourth explanation—climate change—may have dealt a deadly blow. There is evidence that the climate warmed and then suddenly cooled as the Permian drew to a close, which would have made life difficult for animals on land and in the sea. With falling sea levels and volcanic eruptions thrown into the equation, the result may have been the cataclysm that the fossil record shows.

THE AGE OF REPTILES

The Mesozoic Era—between 245 and 66 million years ago—was the time when reptiles became the unchallenged rulers of life on Earth. The dinosaurs became the largest plant eaters and predators to exist on land, and other groups of reptiles successfully conquered the seas and took to the skies. Divided into three periods—the Triassic, Jurassic, and Cretaceous—the Mesozoic saw immense changes on the face of the earth. Sea levels rose and fell, and Pangaea, the giant supercontinent, slowly broke up. The Mesozoic Era ended with the most famous of all mass extinctions.

THE TRIASSIC PERIOD

AT THE BEGINNING OF THE TRIASSIC PERIOD ANIMAL LIFE WAS EMERGING FROM THE AFTERMATH OF THE PERMIAN MASS EXTINCTION. BY THE TIME THE TRIASSIC ENDED, THE FIRST DINOSAURS HAD APPEARED.

The Triassic Period gets its name from the Latin word for "three," because it was first identified from three layers of rock found in Germany. At the start of the Triassic, about 245 million years ago, most of the world's land was still locked together in the supercontinent Pangaea, but as the Triassic came to an end Pangaea began to break apart. Until this happened, land filled much of the Western Hemisphere, and sea levels were at record lows. Across most of Pangaea the climate was warm and dry, but it cooled as the northern and southern continents began to move apart.

▷ *In the heart of Pangaea moisture-loving plants create a splash of greenery in an arid landscape. In Triassic times these plants included tree ferns and horsetails, and also conifers, which often grew on drier ground. These ribbons of green were vital for plant-eating reptiles—and for the meat-eating animals that stalked them.*

THERAPSIDS IN DECLINE
The Triassic world was not unlike the earth in Permian times. Instead of being kept separate by the sea, land animals could roam all over, and fossils of the same species are found in places far apart. The therapsids, which had evolved during the Permian, made full use of this freedom to spread. Fossils of one plant-eating species—a barrel-shaped animal called *Lystrosaurus* (page 61) —have been found in places as far apart as Europe and Antarctica, providing evidence that these continents were once joined.

However, for therapsids as a whole the Triassic period brought difficult times. Although they dominated life on land during the Permian, they failed to maintain their position after the great extinction that brought the Permian to a close. A group of reptiles, the archosaurs, went through a rapid burst of evolution, consigning the therapsids to a dwindling share of the stage. During their decline the therapsids gave rise to the earliest mammals, but these remained small and unobtrusive. They stayed that way for millions of years, until the Age of Reptiles came to its violent end.

THE RULING REPTILES
The first archosaurs—or ruling reptiles—appeared just before the beginning of the Triassic from long-bodied animals that looked like crocodiles, but which were often adapted for life on land. Unlike earlier reptiles, their hind legs were usually longer than their front legs, and they evolved specialized ankles that allowed them to walk with a more upright posture, instead of sprawling with their legs out to the side.

Early offshoots of the archosaur line included *Tanystropheus* (page 60), a fish eater with a bizarrely long neck, and *Scaphonyx* (page 63), a beaked lizard, or rhynchosaur. By the Late Triassic archosaurs themselves went on to become a much more diverse collection of animals. Among them were a host of new reptile groups, including the pterosaurs, or flying reptiles, the dinosaurs, and the crocodilians—the only one of these groups that has survived to the present day.

In Triassic times most archosaurs were predators, and they included some fearsome animals such as *Saurosuchus* (page 63). Although *Saurosuchus* was not a dinosaur, its impressive size provided a hint of what the future held. By comparison, the earliest dinosaurs themselves were sometimes surprisingly small—*Eoraptor* (pages 86–87), for example, which dates back to the Late Triassic, was just 3.3 ft. (1m) long.

MARINE GIANTS
In Triassic times reptiles included nothosaurs—lizardlike animals that probably spent much of their time on the shore—and pistosaurs, which had paddles rather than claws. One group of reptiles, the ichthyosaurs, had become as well-adapted for ocean life as whales and dolphins are today. *Shonisaurus* (page 193), a Late Triassic species, was the largest reptile afloat, weighing perhaps as much as 20 tons.

◁ Sharovipteryx was one of the first vertebrates to take to the air, gliding from tree to tree. It had large rear wings, and possibly a smaller front pair to steer.

This bizarre reptile may have fished from rocks. It belonged to a group of reptiles called prolacertiforms, which died out when the Triassic came to an end.

MAXIMUM LENGTH	9.8 ft. (3m)
TIME	Mid Triassic
FOSSIL FINDS	Europe (Germany), Asia (Israel)

PROTEROSUCHUS
This animal is the earliest archosaur for which complete fossilized skeletons have been found. Like today's crocodiles, it had sprawling legs, and it probably spent much of its time in water, catching fish and other animals with its powerful jaws. It had sharp, conical teeth, and there were secondary teeth in the roof of its mouth—a feature shared by other early archosaurs, but lost as they evolved.

MAXIMUM LENGTH	6.6 ft. (2m)
TIME	Early Triassic
FOSSIL FINDS	Africa (South Africa), Asia (China)

TRIASSIC ANIMALS

During the Triassic Period reptiles strengthened their hold of life on land. Dinosaurs appeared in the Late Triassic, but until then an array of different reptiles competed for supremacy. Many were carnivores, hunting other reptiles, fish, or smaller forms of life; others had teeth or sharp-edged jaws that had evolved for cropping plants. With the rise of the archosaurs, these forerunners of today's mammals found themselves increasingly threatened.

▷ Like other early archosaurs, Proterosuchus *probably lowered its underside onto the ground when resting, raising it to move.*

▽ Tanystropheus *may have used its extraordinary neck to catch fish without having to enter the water.*

TANYSTROPHEUS
Tanystropheus was one of the most remarkable vertebrates of all time. Its head was small, but its slender neck was longer than the rest of its body. The front and rear of its body look so dissimilar that when the first fragmentary fossils were found, they were thought to belong to two entirely different animals. *Tanystropheus'* neck had only 13 vertebrae in some species and as few as 9 in others, which would have limited its ability to bend.

SHAROVIPTERYX
Discovered in the early 1970s, this extraordinary animal is one of the earliest known gliding reptiles and also one of the strangest. Attached to its hind legs, and perhaps its front legs as well, were flaps of elastic skin, which could be stretched out to form wings. Its main wings were positioned at the rear of its body, so its tail would have been crucial for staying balanced in midair.

MAXIMUM LENGTH	49 ft. (15m)
TIME	Late Triassic
FOSSIL FINDS	Russia

ERYTHROSUCHUS
Meaning "red crocodile," *Erythrosuchus* was a close relative of *Proterosuchus*, but better adapted to hunting prey on land. One of the

largest land-based predators of the Early Triassic, it it weighed half a ton and had a head of about 3.3 ft. (1m) long. *Erythrosuchus* would have fed mainly on plant eaters, including therapsids such as *Lystrosaurus*, grasping and killing them with its large, backward-curving teeth.

MAXIMUM LENGTH 6.6 ft. (2m)
TIME Early Triassic
FOSSIL FINDS Africa (South Africa)

TICINOSUCHUS

Fossils of this archosaur show an animal that was well equipped for running after fast-moving prey. Although its body was crocodile-like, it had legs that were upright instead of sprawling and feet with fully developed ankles and heels. This foot anatomy was important because by lifting its heels, it could push down its feet, giving the leverage needed to run.

MAXIMUM LENGTH 9.8 ft. (3m)
TIME Mid Triassic
FOSSIL FINDS Europe (Switzerland)

LYSTROSAURUS

Unlike the other animals on these two pages, *Lystrosaurus* belonged to a group of plant-eating therapsids called dicynodonts, which evolved in the Late Permian period, becoming extinct at the end of the Triassic. It had only two teeth, which grew in its upper jaw. It cut through its food with a sharp-edged beak in much the same way that tortoises do today.

MAXIMUM LENGTH 3.3 ft. (1m)
TIME Early Triassic
FOSSIL FINDS Africa (South Africa), Asia (India, China, Russia), Antarctica

◁ Ticinosuchus' *upright stance was similar to that of later dinosaurs.*

▽ *As well as moving its lower jaw up and down,* Lystrosaurus *could slide it backward to slice through giant horsetails.*

61

THE AGE OF REPTILES

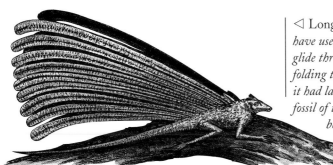

◁ Longisquama *may have used its scales to glide through forests, folding them back when it had landed. Only one fossil of this animal has been found.*

LONGISQUAMA

Ever since its fossilized remains were found in 1969, debate has raged over this small and enigmatic reptile. *Longisquama* had a lizardlike body, with two rows of what look like feathers fastened to its back. If they are true feathers, as some experts believe, it suggests that this animal is a direct ancestor of birds (page 132) and may have been able to fly. However, most paleontologists are not convinced. They believe that the feathers are actually long scales, which may have been used by the animal to regulate its temperature or to disply during courtship. *Longisquama*'s mouth was lined with small, sharp teeth, suggesting that it might have fed on insects.

MAXIMUM LENGTH 6 in. (15cm)
TIME Late Triassic
FOSSIL FINDS Asia (Turkestan)

▽ *Lightly built, fast on its feet, and armed with sharp, backward-curving teeth,* Euparkeria *was well equipped for hunting and killing. The bony plates running down its back protected it from larger predators, although its first defense would have been to run away on its back legs.*

STAGONOLEPIS

With its short legs and long, scaly body, *Stagonolepis* looked like an early crocodile, as did many other early archosaurs. But instead of having long jaws that match a predatory life, it had short ones shaped for feeding on plants. Its teeth were peglike and were positioned at the back of its mouth. The end of its snout was shaped like a trowel, which suggests that it may have rooted for food on or beneath the ground. *Stagonolepis* was slow moving but had armored scales that would have helped protect it from attack.

MAXIMUM LENGTH 9.8 ft. (3m)
TIME Late Triassic
FOSSIL FINDS Europe (Scotland)

EUPARKERIA

Like *Stagonolepis*, this slender-bodied archosaur also bore some resemblance to a small-scale crocodile, with viciously toothed jaws, a series of bony scales along its back, and a long, powerful tail. But its legs were unlike a crocodile's, partly because they were more upright, but also because the hind legs were significantly larger than

the front pair. This difference makes it very likely that *Euparkeria* could run on two legs, either to escape danger or to catch its prey. This way of moving was rare in early reptiles but became widespread when dinosaurs evolved.

MAXIMUM LENGTH 2 ft. (60cm)
TIME Late Triassic
FOSSIL FINDS Africa (South Africa)

LAGOSUCHUS

The remains of four skeletons, missing only parts of the skull, show that *Lagosuchus* was a slender, long-legged, and long-tailed archosaur, which could probably raise itself up on its back legs to run. Its elongated shinbones, combined with its light build, mean that it would have been an effective sprinter, allowing it to catch insects and small reptiles. Its feet were also shaped for speed. They had long metatarsals (bones that form part of the sole in human feet), and these were carried off the ground, helping increase the length of the stride.

MAXIMUM LENGTH 17.7 in. (45cm)

TIME Mid Triassic

FOSSIL FINDS South America (Argentina)

SCAPHONYX

Scaphonyx was a typical rhynchosaur, a plant-eating relative of the archosaurs, with a barrel-shaped body, a narrow beak equipped with tusks, and highly unusual teeth. The teeth on each side of the upper jaws formed a flat plate with a central groove, and the teeth in the lower jaw were pointed and pressed into the groove when the mouth was closed. Most paleontologists think that rhynchosaurs used these strange teeth to eat plants, chopping them up with a scissorlike action and perhaps digging up roots with their tusks. Rhynchosaur fossils have been found on every continent except Australia, and their numbers suggest they were as common as grazing mammals today.

MAXIMUM LENGTH 6.6 ft. (2m)

TIME Mid Triassic

FOSSIL FINDS South America (Brazil)

△ Lagosuchus *had elongated feet, with only its toes touching the ground. This anatomy was common in carnivorous dinosaurs, as well as many mammals.*

SAUROSUCHUS

Weighing up to 2 tons, this archosaur was one of the largest land-based predators in Late Triassic times. Its head alone was up to 3.3 ft. (1m) long and armed with teeth like a crocodile's to tear chunks of flesh from its prey. Although not a dinosaur, *Saurosuchus* showed some striking similarities to tyrannosaurs and other hunters, particularly in the shape of its jaws and teeth and in the way its legs were arranged almost vertically beneath its body. Unlike a tyrannosaur, it moved mainly on all fours, but it is likely that it could run on its back legs alone to launch an attack. *Saurosuchus* belonged to a group of archosaurs called rauisuchids, which also included *Ticinosuchus* (page 61). These animals were an early example of the

▷ Scaphonyx *and its relatives were stoutly built animals that rooted around for vegetable matter—they were the Triassic equivalent of pigs. These stocky planteaters would have been ideal and tasty prey for* Saurosuchus.

increasing size in reptiles, which gathered momentum as the Triassic Period neared its end.

MAXIMUM LENGTH 23 ft. (7m)

TIME Late Triassic

FOSSIL FINDS South America (Argentina, Brazil)

EARLY DINOSAURS

THE FIRST DINOSAURS EVOLVED IN THE LATE
TRIASSIC—OVER 15 MILLION YEARS AFTER
THE AGE OF REPTILES BEGAN. RARE AT FIRST,
THEY BECAME THE LEADING LAND ANIMALS
BY THE TIME THE JURASSIC PERIOD BEGAN.

Studies of dinosaur anatomy show that they all share several key features, which means that they must have evolved from a single ancestor. That ancestor was almost certainly a thecodont, or primitive archosaur, which gave rise to a new line of reptiles that could walk on two legs. How and when this line split into the ornithischians and saurischians is not yet known, but the result was a range of reptiles that developed major differences in body shape and ways of life.

Early dinosaurs walked with just three of their toes in contact with the ground, rather than four or five. As a result, three-toed footprints are strong evidence of dinosaurs on the move. One or two specimens have been dated back to the Early Triassic, but most paleontologists are unconvinced. The earliest reliable dinosaur footprints date to the Late Triassic—the time Herrerasaurus *and* Eoraptor *were alive.*

EARLY DAYS

Proterosuchus (page 60) looked much more like a crocodile than a dinosaur—but in fact, both crocodiles and dinosaurs evolved from animals like this. While crocodiles kept *Proterosuchus'* sprawling four-legged gait, the dinosaurs developed differently. Their back legs became larger than their front legs, and the femur, or thighbone, evolved a sharp bend near the point where it joined the rest of the body. Also, the head of the femur developed a ball-like shape, fitting into a socket in the hip. These changes added up to one thing: a new group of carnivorous reptiles that could stand upright on their back legs, instead of moving on legs that sprawled out toward their sides.

Dinosaurs had several features that help to separate them from other reptiles. Among these were a reduced number of bones in the fourth finger (if present) and hip sockets that had a central hole, or window. By contrast, typical hip sockets—including human ones—are closed, like a cup.

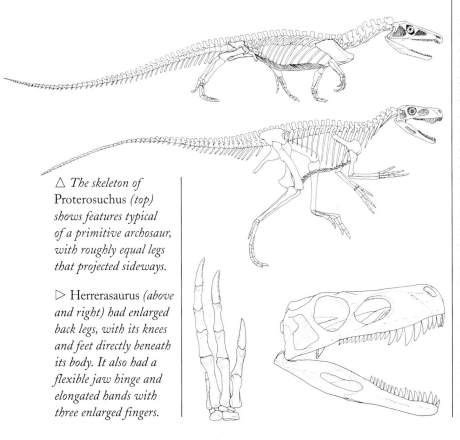

△ *The skeleton of* Proterosuchus *(top) shows features typical of a primitive archosaur, with roughly equal legs that projected sideways.*

▷ Herrerasaurus *(above and right) had enlarged back legs, with its knees and feet directly beneath its body. It also had a flexible jaw hinge and elongated hands with three enlarged fingers.*

WORLDWIDE HUNT

Where these animals first appeared is still not clear, partly because most of the world's land was joined together in Triassic times. But Argentina's so-called Wild West has produced a clutch of fossils that include some of the earliest dinosaurs on record. Fragments of one *Herrerasaurus* were found in the 1950s, followed by a partial skeleton in 1988 that showed that *Herrerasaurus* was a bipedal carnivore up to 19.7 ft. (6m) long, with long jaws and backward-curving teeth. It resembled a theropod (page 113), with long-fingered hands for grasping prey.

In 1991 the same part of the world produced fossils of *Eoraptor*, or "dawn thief," a bipedal hunter just 3.3 ft. (1m) long. *Eoraptor* lived about 228 million years ago and was less specialized than *Herrerasaurus*, thus even closer to the original protodinosaur. But in 1999 paleontologists working in Madagascar found jawbones of two even earlier dinosaurs, provisionally dated at more than 230 million years old. The bones showed that these dinosaurs were not carnivores, but plant eaters called prosauropods, which some thought had evolved from meat-eating ancestors.

CHANGING TIMES

The existence of plant-eating dinosaurs so long ago shows that dinosaurs were already diversifying as the Mid Triassic ended and the Late Triassic began. Many existing animal groups, such as the mammallike reptiles, or therapsids, either declined or disappeared. Dinosaurs may have triggered this change by outcompeting existing animals. Another possibility is that the world's climate might have abruptly altered, triggering a wave of extinctions and clearing the way for dinosaurs to expand.

◁ *Herrerasaurus may have been an early theropod—a group that included all the predatory dinosaurs. The bipedal posture was effective for hunting, and in Cretaceous times theropods included the largest carnivores that have ever lived.*

▽ *Known from many well-preserved fossils,* Plateosaurus *was a plant-eating prosauropod that lived in the Late Triassic. Compared to the small prosauropods recently found in Madagascar, it was a large animal, about 23 ft. (7m) long. Prosauropods looked similar to sauropods (page 71), but had feet with long toes.*

THE JURASSIC PERIOD

FAMOUS FOR ITS DINOSAURS, THE JURASSIC PERIOD WAS AN EVENTFUL TIME FOR REPTILIAN LIFE AS A WHOLE. FOR THE FIRST TIME REPTILES DOMINATED LIFE ON LAND, IN THE SEA, AND IN THE AIR.

Named after a chain of mountains in Europe, the Jurassic started about 208 million years ago. Compared to the Triassic Period, it was a time of great change in the earth's crust, as the giant supercontinent of Pangaea began to break up. The climate became wetter and warmer, and sea levels rose, flooding large areas of low-lying land. For animal life these changes created new opportunities. On land a moister climate meant that plant food was easier to find; in the sea warm shallows created perfect conditions for coral reefs.

▷ *Average temperatures were warm in the Jurassic, with little or no ice at the poles. This scene shows a typical Jurassic landscape, dominated by forests of conifers, with scattered cycads and tree ferns. Dinosaurs probably scattered cycad seeds, just as mammals today scatter the seeds of some plants.*

A PARTING OF WAYS
With the breakup of Pangaea the continents began their long journey into the positions they occupy today. The Atlantic Ocean started to form, and North and South America split apart. These changes had an important effect on land animals, because it meant that they could no longer mix freely. Instead, each continent began to develop its own characteristic wildlife—a feature that became more pronounced the longer they remained apart. The separation can often be seen through fossil evidence. For example, giant sauropods lived in both North and South America during the Jurassic, but each continent had its own particular kinds—neither is found in both.

DINOSAURS IN THE ASCENDANT
When the Jurassic Period began dinosaurs had established themselves as the prominent animals on land. They had already split into several lines, and most of these were set to continue for nearly 150 million years, until the Age of Reptiles abruptly came to an end. However, there were some casualties along the way. Among the sauropods, for example, the cetiosaur family died out at the end of the Jurassic, and several other dinosaur families disappeared.

The warm and humid conditions that lasted for most of the Jurassic were ideal for large plant eaters to evolve, because there was a vast supply of food. And as plant eaters increased in size, so did the animals that preyed upon them. From relatively modest beginnings predatory dinosaurs evolved into giants such as *Megalosaurus*, which was up to 29.5 ft. (9m) long. Outwardly *Megalosaurus* was similar to the better known tyrannosaurs, but it evolved millions of years before they appeared.

These huge predators had no natural enemies, but not all dinosaurs were built on a giant scale. *Compsognathus*, which lived in the Late Jurassic, was also a hunter, but it weighed only about 6.6 lb. (3kg).

LIFE IN THE SEA AND AIR
During the Jurassic several new families of marine reptiles appeared. Among them were the long-necked plesiosaurs and elasmosaurs and also the pliosaurs, which included some of the largest predators to live in the seas. Marine life was particularly rich in the Jurassic, because sea levels were generally higher than they are today. Sunlit shallows rich in sediment teemed with mollusks and other small animals.

In the air even greater changes were underway. The first flying reptiles, or pterosaurs, had evolved in the Late Triassic, and during the Jurassic they took command of the skies on their leathery wings. But from a branch of the dinosaur world—the theropods—a completely new group of flying animals came into being. Instead of flying on wings of skin, they used feathers (page 133), and they rapidly diversified as the Jurassic came to its end. We know them as birds—the only dinosaurs still in existence today.

THE CRETACEOUS PERIOD

A TIME OF DRAMATIC SHIFTS IN THE WORLD'S CONTINENTS, TOGETHER WITH RECORD SEA LEVELS, THE CRETACEOUS PERIOD SAW AN EXPLOSIVE GROWTH IN LIFE—ONE THAT CAME TO A CATACLYSMIC END.

The Cretaceous Period began 144 million years ago when the supercontinent of Pangaea had broken up. Two major fragments—Laurasia in the north and Gondwana in the south—began cracking up as well, to form the continents that exist today. These continental movements produced major changes in the earth's climate and sea levels up to 660 ft. (200m) higher than they are now. Microscopic life abounded in the seas, and tiny shells built up in vast banks on the ocean floor, eventually turning into chalk. Known in Latin as *creta*, chalk gave the Cretaceous its name.

▷ With volcanoes erupting in the distance, Late Cretaceous plants bloom to attract pollinating insects. Volcanic activity was a feature of the Cretaceous Period, and average temperatures were much higher than they are today. Subtropical landscapes—like the one shown here—extended as far north as present-day New York City.

LIFE ON LAND
Unlike the Triassic or Jurassic Periods, the Cretaceous was similar in some ways to the world we know today. Flowering plants probably evolved in the Late Jurassic or Early Cretaceous, but it was during the Cretaceous that they really began to make their mark. These plants included the first broad-leaved trees, which slowly ousted conifers in many parts of the world. As flowering plants evolved, so did pollinating insects such as bees. It was the start of a phenomenally successful partnership, which continues to the present day.

The Cretaceous landscape was also home to mammals, which had clung on to life throughout Jurassic times. Like their Jurassic forebears they were still small, and they avoided direct competition with reptiles by foraging for food at night. They included primitive marsupials, which raised their young in a pouch, as well as some pocket-size placentals—species that grew their young inside their bodies, as most mammals do today. There were birds, but much more evident were pterosaurs—a sign that the reign of reptiles was still at its height. The Cretaceous also produced the largest, fastest, and most intelligent dinosaurs that the world had yet seen.

LATE ARRIVALS
By the beginning of the Cretaceous dinosaurs had a history dating back over 80 million years. During this long finale of the reptile age several new groups of dinosaurs came into being, and others rapidly expanded. They included the armored dinosaurs, the duck-billed dinosaurs, or hadrosaurs, and the titanosaurs—a group of southern sauropods that may have included the heaviest dinosaurs. Apart from these plant eaters, the Late Cretaceous also saw the arrival of the tyrannosaurs, a meat-eating family that included the largest land predators ever to have stalked the earth.

In the seas reptiles still held sway. They included plesiosaurs and ichthyosaurs, which had existed throughout the Jurassic, and a new group—the mosasaurs, giant marine lizards that became the dominant oceangoing reptiles as the Cretaceous neared its end. Turtles were common, having changed little in over 200 million years. They all shared the seas with fish known as teleosts. These fish had thinner and lighter scales than earlier fish, making them faster and more maneuverable.

END OF THE CRETACEOUS
If the Cretaceous world had continued, reptiles might still be the earth's dominant animals, and mammals might have died out. But 66 million years ago something happened that devastated life on land and in the sea, sweeping aside all of the dinosaurs and many other reptiles as well. Most experts now believe that this catastrophe was caused by an impact from outer space (page 204), but other factors—such as volcanic eruptions—may have already set the process in motion. In any event, with this multiple catastrophe the Mesozoic Era ended, and the great Age of Reptiles was over.

		Cambrian	Ordovician	Silurian	Devonian	Carboniferous	Permian	Triassic

THE TERTIARY PERIOD

DINOSAUR GROUPS

Early in their evolution dinosaurs split into two groups: the ornithischians, or bird-hipped dinosaurs, and the saurischians, or lizard-hipped dinosaurs. As well as a different hip anatomy, these two groups developed other distinctive features and different ways of life. The ornithischians were plant eaters and walked either on four legs or on two. The saurischians included the plant-eating sauropods, which walked on all fours, and all the predatory dinosaurs, or theropods, which were almost entirely bipedal. Birds are actually descended from lizard-hipped dinosaurs, and they are the only members of the two troups alive today.

Bird-hipped
dinosaur
(ornithischian)

Lizard-hipped
dinosaur
(saurischian)

△ In bird-hipped dinosaurs two hipbones—the ischium and pubis—pointed backward and were close together. In lizard-hipped dinosaurs the two bones pointed in different directions.

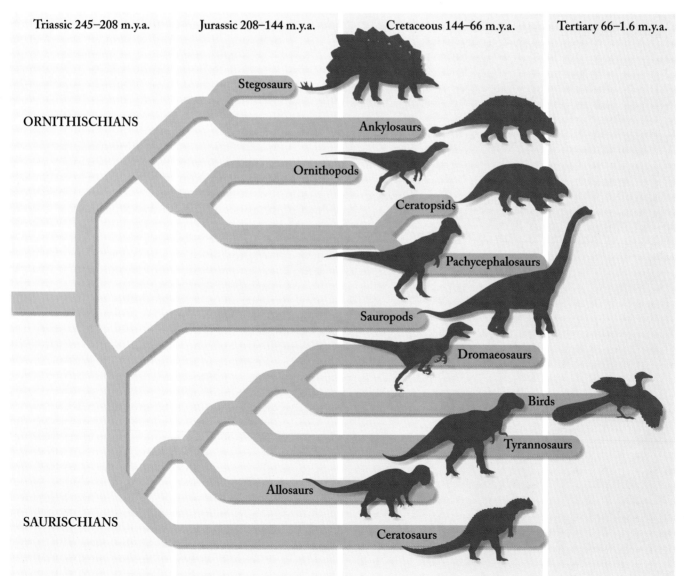

Triassic 245–208 m.y.a.   Jurassic 208–144 m.y.a.   Cretaceous 144–66 m.y.a.   Tertiary 66–1.6 m.y.a.

ORNITHISCHIANS

Stegosaurs

Ankylosaurs

Ornithopods

Ceratopsids

Pachycephalosaurs

Sauropods

Dromaeosaurs

Birds

Tyrannosaurs

Allosaurs

SAURISCHIANS

Ceratosaurs

70

PLANT-EATING GIANTS

With their gigantic necks and barrel-shaped bodies, the sauropods were the unrivaled giants of the dinosaur world. These slow-moving plant eaters evolved during the Jurassic Period, and over the next 50 million years they developed into the largest land animals the world has ever seen. Some of them tipped the scales at over 80 tons—close to the limit for any animal that moves on legs. There were several families of sauropods, including cetiosaurs, brachiosaurs, diplodocids, and titanosaurs, and they processed almost unbelievable amounts of plant food.

GIANTS AMONG GIANTS

A carnosaur, Ceratosaurus *(page 117), lurks menacingly on a hillside overlooking a herd of* Apatosaurus *(pages 80–81) as the gentle diplodocids munch their way through a forest. Diplodocids probably used their long, whiplike tails and their massive forelimbs to defend themselves against attack from such predatory carnosaurs.*

PLANT-EATING GIANTS

CETIOSAURS

Cetiosaurs were among the first sauropods, dating back to the Early Jurassic, and they were also the first to be discovered. Their huge bodies were supported by four pillarlike legs, and they had very small heads, but extremely long necks and tails. They grazed on trees and low-growing plants, swallowing their food whole, because like most plant-eating dinosaurs, they were not able to chew. The cetiosaur family shared a key characteristic— vertebrae that were almost solid. This feature is a primitive one, and as sauropods evolved their backbones became increasingly hollowed out as a way of saving weight.

OMEISAURUS
Identified in 1939, this Chinese cetiosaur was named after the mountain where its fossils were found. Fragments of most parts of its skeleton have been discovered, giving us a very good picture of what it looked like. *Omeisaurus* had a long neck, a small, wedge-shaped head, and a slightly forward-sloping gait, with its hips higher than its shoulders. Its tail was relatively short, although still huge by today's standards, and it may have had a clubbed tip, though this may not have been a feature of all species. Like all sauropods, *Omeisaurus* did not simply trail its tail on the ground. Instead, it probably held its tail almost horizontal when on the move, using it as a counterbalance or even as a weapon.

MAXIMUM LENGTH	50 ft (15m)
TIME	Late Jurassic
FOSSIL FINDS	Asia (China)

CETIOSAURUS
The first fossils of *Cetiosaurus* were found in the early 1800s, several decades before the existence of dinosaurs became known. Its name, which means "whale lizard," was given to it in 1841—one of many examples of dinosaur remains being confused with those of other animals. It was originally thought to be some kind of giant marine reptile, until it was finally recognized as a dinosaur in 1869. *Cetiosaurus* was a massive animal, weighing up to 27 tons. It had a relatively short neck and tail, but its legs were impressive—its thighbones were nearly 6.5 ft. (2m) long. Its front and back legs appear to have been roughly the same length, which means that its back would have been almost level. This sets it apart from many later sauropods, which had front and back legs of distinctly different lengths. No traces of a skull have been found, so scientists do not know how it ate, but its teeth probably worked like a rake, allowing it to strip leaves off of trees and other plants.

MAXIMUM LENGTH	60 ft. (18m)
TIME	Mid to Late Jurassic
FOSSIL FINDS	Europe (England), Africa (Morocco)

◁ Omeisaurus *was almost certainly a herd-forming animal. Despite its size, it was vulnerable to predators and needed the protection that came from living in groups.*

CETIOSAURS

◁ *For many years* Cetiosaurus *was the largest land animal known to science. Since then many other sauropod fossils have been discovered. They show that, despite its great size,* Cetiosaurus *was actually a middleweight member of the sauropod group.*

BARAPASAURUS

This animal is the oldest sauropod discovered so far. Its exact classification is uncertain, but it was a massively built animal, equal to *Cetiosaurus* in size and weight or possibly even heavier. Six partial skeletons of *Barapasaurus* have been uncovered, as well as a number of less complete remains, but so far none includes skulls or feet. However, paleontologists have found fossilized teeth—spoon-shaped with serrated edges and ideal for tearing off leaves. *Barapasaurus* shows that sauropods were already very large animals near the beginning of the Jurassic. Some scientists classify this animal in a separate family of very primitive sauropods, called the vulcanodontids. The founding member of this family, called *Vulcanodon*, was found in Africa.

MAXIMUM LENGTH 60 ft. (18m)

TIME Early Jurassic

FOSSIL FINDS Asia (India)

HAPLOCANTHOSAURUS

Haplocanthosaurus is the most primitive sauropod that has been discovered in North America, with the first known fossils being unearthed about a century ago. It had a long neck and tail and showed similarities to the brachiosaurs (page 76) and the diplodocids (page 80). Establishing its exact place in classification is not easy, because as with many other cetiosaurs, no skull remains have been found. In evolutionary terms *Haplocanthosaurus* seems to have been something of a throwback. It lived toward the end of the Jurassic Period, a time when most

other cetiosaurs had died out, and has been described as a living fossil of its time.

MAXIMUM LENGTH 73 ft. (22m)

TIME Late Jurassic

FOSSIL FINDS North America

▽ Barapasaurus *is the earliest known sauropod. Its weight may have been as much as 30 tons.*

SHUNOSAURUS

Compared to some cetiosaurs, this Chinese dinosaur is a recent discovery—the first fossil find dating back to 1977. Measuring just 33 ft. (10m) long, it was almost petite by sauropod standards and probably weighed no more than a fully grown female elephant. Another interesting feature is the tip of its tail. This ended in a bony club, which would have made a very effective weapon. A similar defense system appeared later in a different group of plant eaters—the ankylosaurs (page 164). Over 20 discoveries of almost complete *Shunosaurus* skeletons have been found, giving an unusually good picture of what this animal looked like. Compared to most sauropods, the nostrils were positioned low down on its muzzle, and it had relatively small teeth with elongated crowns.

MAXIMUM LENGTH 33 ft. (10m)

TIME Mid Jurassic

FOSSIL FINDS Asia (China)

△ *By flicking its tail like a whip,* Shunosaurus *would have been able to inflict a deadly blow with its tail club. The spikes in the club were extensions of the bones inside the tail.*

75

PLANT-EATING GIANTS

BRACHIOSAURS AND CAMARASAURS

The brachiosaurs were spectacularly long-necked sauropods, the camarasaurs were smaller, with shorter necks and tails. Although both groups were plant eaters, differences in their body shape and in the design of their teeth mean that they were unlikely to have eaten the same food. Brachiosaurs had remarkably long front legs, and their teeth were shaped like chisels. Camarasaurs looked more like other sauropods, but they had forward-pointing teeth set in an unusual bulldoglike snout.

◁ *Brachiosaurus was the dinosaur equivalent of the giraffe, but on a much larger scale. Its blood pressure was exceptionally high; this made sure oxygen reached its brain.*

▽ *Brachiosaurus' neck had a framework of 14 hollow but extremely strong vertebrae. Like the jib of a crane, it raised its head high into the treetops.*

BRACHIOSAURUS

As well as being one of the heaviest dinosaurs, with a weight of up to 80 tons, *Brachiosaurus* is the largest species to have had its skeleton assembled in a museum (page 161). Its front legs were much longer than its hind legs, and this, together with its long neck, allowed it to reach up to 53 ft. (16m), which is more than two and a half times as high as a giraffe. Its head was relatively small, with large, upward-facing nostrils that opened in a dome on top of its head. At one time, paleontologists thought that *Brachiosaurus'* nostrils showed that it fed in lakes. However, this is unlikely to be true, because its lungs would have collapsed if they were more than about 10 ft. underwater. Despite its huge size, *Brachiosaurus* may not have been the largest member of its family. In 1994 an American team unearthed fossils of a bigger animal, *Sauroposeidon*, which stood over 60 ft. (18m) tall.

MAXIMUM LENGTH	85 ft. (26m)
TIME	Mid to Late Jurassic
FOSSIL FINDS	North America, Africa, Europe (Portugal)

CAMARASAURUS

Weighing about 20 tons, *Camarasaurus* was much more compact than *Brachiosaurus*. Many fossils of this dinosaur have been found, including several complete skeletons, which, for a sauropod, makes this species almost unique. *Camarasaurus* would probably have lived in herds for protection, although like *Brachiosaurus*, it could have lashed out at its enemies with extra-long claws on its thumbs. *Camarasaurus* had large nostrils and may have had a keen sense of smell. Its boxlike head and the size of its nostrils have led some scientists to suggest that it had an elephantlike trunk. However, trunks are made entirely from soft tissue, which very rarely shows up in fossils. As a result this intriguing idea, which has been suggested for other sauropods, is very difficult to prove.

MAXIMUM LENGTH	60 ft. (18m)
TIME	Late Jurassic
FOSSIL FINDS	North America (U.S.A.), Europe (Portugal)

OPISTHOCOELICAUDIA

The only known skeleton of this sauropod, minus its head and neck, was found in 1965. As a result its exact appearance is still a matter of guesswork, and so is its place in the sauropod world. It had one highly distinctive feature: tail vertebrae that were hollowed out behind, rather than in front, which is the more normal pattern for sauropods. This arrangement would have made its tail unusually strong, allowing *Opisthocoelicaudia* to rear up on its hind legs, using its tail as a prop.

MAXIMUM LENGTH	16.5 ft. (5m)
TIME	Late Cretaceous
FOSSIL FINDS	Central Asia

EUHELOPUS

Smaller than *Camarasaurus* but similar in overall shape, *Euhelopus* would never have crossed paths with its American relative, because it lived in the Far East. Its neck was much longer, and its head was also longer and more pointed, although still with a steeply sloping front. *Euhelopus* had up to 19 neck vertebrae, unlike *Camarasaurus*, which had 12—one reason why it is sometimes classified in a separate family.

MAXIMUM LENGTH	50 ft. (15m)
TIME	Late Jurassic
FOSSIL FINDS	Asia (China)

▽ Camarasaurus *(top)* means "chambered lizard." It gets its name from the hollow chambers in its vertebrae, which kept it light for its size. Its neck was relatively short.

▽ Opisthocoelicaudia *(middle)* may have been a camarasaur, but some paleontologists think it is more likely to have been a titanosaur *(page 88)*.

▽ Euhelopus *(bottom)* probably weighed 15-20 tons. It had teeth all around its jaws. Many other sauropods had them only in the front.

FEEDING ON PLANTS

ALTHOUGH THE EARLIEST DINOSAURS WERE HUNTERS, PLANT-EATING SPECIES STEADILY OUTNUMBERED THEM AS THE AGE OF REPTILES WORE ON. MANY COULD NOT CHEW—THEY SWALLOWED THEIR FOOD WHOLE.

When the first plant-eating dinosaurs evolved, in the Late Triassic, there were no flowering plants, so there was no grass. Instead of grazing, like many of today's hooved mammals, early plant-eating dinosaurs fed on coniferous trees and other plants with tough foliage and tall trunks or stems. The same was true for most of the Jurassic Period, but during the Cretaceous flowering plants became widespread. They created a carpet of succulent, low-growing foliage, which made it easier to feed at or near ground level.

▷ *Ferns, cycads, and horsetails (left to right) were important foods for dinosaurs in the Jurassic.*

▽ *Magnolias were among the first flowering plants. Compared to other prehistoric plants, their leaves were juicy and nutritious.*

These fossilized stones are gastroliths, or stomach stones, from a plant-eating dinosaur find. Dinosaurs swallowed these to help them grind their food—an important digestive aid for animals often lacking chewing teeth. The food would travel through the digestive system, but the stones, being heavier, stayed behind. Crocodiles, ostriches, and some other birds do the same thing today.

A CHANGING MENU

Plant-eating dinosaurs evolved in step with the vegetation around them. During the Triassic and Jurassic most had long necks to allow them to browse high off the ground. They may also have used their necks like horizontal booms so that they could crop wide areas of shorter plants, but

many paleontologists doubt that this was common. There was probably not enough of this vegetation to make low-level feeding worthwhile. With the evolution of flowering plants, this began to change. For the first time there was plenty of plant food close to the ground, and because flowering plants tended to be faster-growing, they recovered quickly after being eaten. This new food supply was quite different from the plant cover of the past, and it probably explains why smaller ornithopods (pages 91–112) and armored dinosaurs (pages 151–168) became so widespread in Cretaceous times.

HOW SAUROPODS FED

Plant-eating mammals have two main types of teeth. The incisors, at the front of the jaw, bite off the food, and the molars, near the back, grind it. By comparison, sauropods—by far the largest plant-eating dinosaurs—had a much simpler arrangement. Their teeth formed a matching set, usually in the front of the jaw, and they could collect food, but could not chew it. A sauropod would swallow food whole, which was ground up in its stomach. The plant pulp was then broken down by microbes living in the animal's

▷ *Apatosaurus' muscular stomach worked like a cement mixer. It churned up leaves, branches, and tough cones and broke them into small, easily digested pieces with the help of gastroliths.*

stomach. Once the microbes had done their work, the dinosaur could absorb the nutrients released.

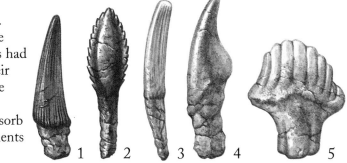

CHEWING TEETH

Ornithopods had a more mammalian way of eating. Many gathered their food using a toothless beak that formed the front of the jaw. They would then move the food to the back of their mouth, where it was sliced or ground up by a battery of specialized teeth. By the time the food arrived in the stomach, it was ready for microbes to break it down. Some bird-hipped dinosaurs had just a handful of teeth, but hadrosaurs (pages 104–107) often had hundreds.

△ *Plant eaters' teeth were usually peglike, although some were flat. They all had an endless supply of teeth throughout their lives. From left to right, these teeth belonged to Heterodontosaurus (1), Plateosaurus (2), Diplodocus (3), Apatosaurus (4), and Stegosaurus (5).*

▽ *A fully grown* Apatosaurus *probably ate under half a ton of food a day—less than one-fiftieth of its body weight. It could survive on this meager diet because it was cold-blooded. Today's warm-blooded plant eaters need a much higher food intake.*

PLANT-EATING DINOSAURS

DIPLODOCIDS

The diplodocids include the longest dinosaurs that are known from complete skeletons. *Diplodocus*, the best-known species, was up to 89 ft. (27m) long, but the partial remains of *Seismosaurus* (page 83) suggest that some diplodocids were even longer than this. If so, they may well have been the longest vertebrates ever to have existed on Earth. Diplodocids were built like living suspension bridges, with pillarlike legs, extraordinarily long necks, and even longer, narrow-tipped tails. Despite their great length, they were not as heavy as many other sauropods, because their skeletons were shaped to save weight. They had elongated heads, large nostrils located on top near their eyes, and unusually small, rodlike teeth.

DIPLODOCUS
Diplodocus means "double beam"—a name that describes this dinosaur's tail. Beneath each of its tail vertebra was a length of bone that ran the length of the tail, stengthening it and protecting the blood vessels inside it. It could lash out with the tip of its tail if it came under attack. *Diplodocus'* remarkable length has led to many questions about how it moved and ate. Some scientists believe that it would have moved with its head held almost horizontal in front and its tail in a similar position at the rear. It is also likely that it could raise itself on its hind legs and lift its head high up into the trees to eat. Like its relatives, *Diplodocus* had teeth only in the front of its mouth.

Apatosaurus

Diplodocus

▷ *The first fossil of* Apatosaurus—*without the skull—was found in 1877, but the first complete skeleton of this dinosaur was not assembled until 1975.*

▷ Diplodocus *had slender teeth that worked like a comb, gathering in the soft parts of plants. It may have fed on low-growing vegetation as well as trees.*

MAXIMUM LENGTH	88.6 ft. (27m)
TIME	Late Jurassic
FOSSIL FINDS	North America (western U.S.A.)

Dicraeosaurus

▷ Dicraeosaurus *was smaller than most diplodocids and probably fed on low-growing plants. Unlike its later relatives, it did not have a whiplike tip to its tail.*

▽ Mamenchisaurus' *neck accounted for half the entire length of its body. It had 19 neck vertebrae. When stretched, they made the neck extra-long.*

Mamenchisaurus

▷ Barosaurus' *thighbone measured up to 8 ft. (2.5m)— taller than an adult man. Its back legs and tail may have acted like a tripod, allowing it to reach high into the trees.*

Barosaurus

APATOSAURUS

Once also known as *Brontosaurus*, *Apatosaurus* was slightly smaller than *Diplodocus* but at 30 tons much more heavily built. As with *Diplodocus* uncertainty surrounds exactly how it lived. For many years scientists have assumed that it could rear up on its hind legs to eat, using its tail as a prop. But some recent research suggests that its neck might have been surprisingly inflexible, so that when it was on all fours, it could raise its head no more than 16.4 ft. (5m) above the ground. *Apatosaurus* probably defended itself by using its tail and the sharp toe claw on each of its front feet. *Apatosaurus* bones have been found with *Allosaurus* teeth marks, but it is not possible to tell whether these giant plant eaters had been attacked while alive or scavenged when already dead.

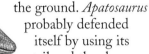

MAXIMUM LENGTH	82 ft. (25m)
TIME	Late Jurassic
FOSSIL FINDS	North America (western U.S.A.)

DICRAEOSAURUS

Dicraeosaurus was a relatively compact diplodocid, and one of the earliest members of the family. Compared to later forms, it had a short neck and tail and a comparatively large head. Its vertebrae also show some peculiarities, with unusual Y-shaped spikes running along the length of the backbone and into the neck. These may have channeled supporting ligaments and would have formed a clearly visible ridge along its spine.

MAXIMUM LENGTH	46 ft. (14m)
TIME	Late Jurassic
FOSSIL FINDS	Africa (Tanzania)

MAMENCHISAURUS

Until the discovery of *Sauroposeidon* in 1994 (page 82), *Mamenchisaurus* held the record for neck length of a dinosaur— an astounding 46 ft. (14m). This cranelike neck may have been used horizontally as much as vertically, allowing *Mamenchisaurus* to reach for plants growing on marshy ground or in dense thickets, while the rest of its body was safely distanced. When this dinosaur was on the move, it probably held its head directly in front of its body, so that its neck was roughly level. Its neck vertebrae were unusually light and thin, with interconnecting rodlike ribs for strength. Its neck was not very flexible and bent mainly at the head and shoulders, rather than in between. Some paleontologists think that *Mamenchisaurus* is so unusual that it should be classified in a family of its own.

MAXIMUM LENGTH	82 ft. (25m)
TIME	Late Jurassic
FOSSIL FINDS	Asia (China)

BAROSAURUS

Barosaurus, which means "heavy lizard," was a huge diplodocid, weighing perhaps as much as 40 tons. Similar in form and structure to *Diplodocus*, but with particularly elongated neck vertebrae, it would have used size as its main defense. Like some of its relatives, *Barosaurus*' center of gravity was far back down its body, a feature that would have helped if it reared up on its back legs to feed from trees. Judging from fossil finds in Africa and North America, this dinosaur was one of the most widespread members of the diplodocid family.

MAXIMUM LENGTH	88.6 ft. (27m)
TIME	Late Jurassic
FOSSIL FINDS	North America (U.S.A.), Africa (Tanzania)

PLANT-EATING GIANTS

▷ *Giant sauropods like* Supersaurus *(on the left) had very similar body structures, even though on a gigantic scale. The exact size and weight of these enormous plant eaters is uncertain because no complete fossils have been found yet. Other contenders for the title of largest dinosaur ever include* Argentinosaurus *(page 88) and a colossal brachiosaur called* Sauroposeidon, *whose remains were found in the grounds of a prison in Oklahoma in 1994.*

AMARGASAURUS

An almost complete skeleton of *Amargasaurus* was discovered in Argentinian Patagonia in 1984. It revealed that this diplodocid had a highly unusual row of vertebral spike, up to 25.6 in. (65cm) long, running along the back of its neck. These may have formed a spiky mane, or they may have been covered in skin, creating a structure like a double sail. Whichever form they took, they were a remarkable feature and may have played a part in the animal's social life, or they may have been used in defense—a valuable plus for an animal that was under half the length of many of its larger cousins. *Amargasaurus* also had a slender, whiplike tail and blunt teeth shaped for stripping foliage from branches. Like other sauropods, it probably swallowed stones or gastroliths (page 78) to help it break down its food. With its spiky vertebrae, *Amargasaurus* is similar to *Dicraeosaurus* (page 81), and some paleontologists classify these two dinosaurs in a family of their own.

MAXIMUM LENGTH	39.4 ft. (12m)
TIME	Early Cretaceous
FOSSIL FINDS	South America (Argentina)

SUPERSAURUS

A giant among giants, *Supersaurus* has the distinction of being one of the largest land animals ever to have walked the earth. The first fossils were discovered in 1972 in Dry Mesa Quarry, Colorado—a site that has produced some of the most spectacular sauropod finds in the world. The *Supersaurus* remains were far from complete, but they included shoulder blades 7.9 ft. (2.4m) long and nearly 3.3 ft. (1m) wide—enough room for two people to lie on, with plenty of legroom to spare. From remains like these paleontologists estimate that *Supersaurus* might have weighed as much as 50 tons. With its head held high, it would have towered 50 ft. (15m) above the ground— higher than the average house. *Supersaurus'* tremendous weight was supported by four pillar-shaped legs, the hind legs being longer than the front ones.

Like other diplodocids, it had elephant-like feet with five toes and a large claw on each front thumb. The claws may have been used as defensive weapons, although its huge tail would have been a more substantial deterrent. Analysis of its fossilized tracks show that it moved slowly—as would be expected for an animal of such size.

MAXIMUM LENGTH	125 ft. (42m)
TIME	Late Jurassic
FOSSIL FINDS	North America (Colorado)

ULTRASAUROS

There are doubts about whether *Ultrasauros* is truly a separate species of dinosaur or whether its remains are actually a mixture from two other dinosaurs—*Supersaurus* and *Brachiosaurus*. The first of these remains, which were found in 1979, came from the same quarry that produced *Supersaurus*, and they include bones that show *Ultrasauros* would have stood about 26.2 ft. (8m) tall at the shoulder, over four times the height of an average man. *Ultrasauros* gets its unusual spelling because scientific names can never be used twice for different animals. It was originally called *Ultrasaurus*, but had to be renamed because the name *Ultrasaurus* had already been used two years earlier for a smaller sauropod found in South Korea.

MAXIMUM LENGTH	100 ft. (30m)
TIME	Late Jurassic
FOSSIL FINDS	North America (Colorado)

SEISMOSAURUS

Known from remains discovered in 1979, *Seismosaurus*, meaning "earthquake lizard," was built on a massive scale. Some estimates put its total length at up to 165 ft. (50m), although 131 ft. (40m) is probably more likely. However, with a weight of perhaps 30 tons, or more than double that according to some calculations, it would have more than lived up to its name. Like other diplodocids, it had extra bones beneath its spine to help support its neck and tail. Its tail had the standard diplodocid whiplike tip, but it also seems to have had a kink—a feature that has not yet been explained. In comparison with the rest of its body its head was tiny—a characteristic feature of sauropods as a whole. Stomach stones, or gastroliths, have been found among *Seismosaurus*' fossilized remains, indicating that it lived on a diet of tough plants that needed to be ground down before they could be digested. The only known fossil of this dinosaur has still not been fully excavated because it lies deeply buried in sandstone. The latest technology—including ground-penetrating radar—has been used to pinpoint the fossilized bones that still remain hidden beneath the surface.

MAXIMUM LENGTH	Up to 165 ft. (50m)
TIME	Late Jurassic
FOSSIL FINDS	North America (New Mexico)

◁ *This reconstruction of* Ultrasauros *(center) is very much an artist's impression because only partial remains of this animal have been found, and they may not even belong to the same animal. If* Ultrasauros *really did exist, its weight might have been well over 50 tons.*

◁ *The only known remains of* Seismosaurus *(on the right) were found when two hikers literally stumbled on the tip of its fossilized tail. When paleontologists began to excavate, the remains they found turned out to be among the largest discovered so far. The fossils show that* Seismosaurus *was a typical diplodocid, but one built on an extra-large scale.*

A QUESTION OF SIZE

HOW HEAVY WERE THE LARGEST DINOSAURS? WHY DID THEY GROW TO SUCH ENORMOUS SIZES? QUESTIONS LIKE THESE ARE EASY TO ASK, BUT AS PALEONTOLOGISTS HAVE DISCOVERED, NOT SO EASY TO ANSWER.

Sauropod dinosaurs were without doubt the largest land animals that have ever lived on Earth, weighing perhaps 15 times as much as any four-legged animal alive today. For biologists and for engineers, these giant plant eaters exert a powerful fascination, because they probably reached the physical proportions that limit animal size. Enormous dimensions must have brought advantages, or these giants would not have evolved, but they would also have created a range of practical problems—ones that evolution had to overcome.

WHY BE LARGE?

There are several reasons why gigantism may have evolved in plant-eating dinosaurs. One is that plant digestion works best on a large scale. Like today's plant eaters, sauropods relied on microbes to break down their food, and the microbes released heat as they worked. This heat helped speed up the process of digestion, and the larger the dinosaur's stomach, the more heat it would have generated. In relative terms giant dinosaurs needed less food for each ton of body weight, as they used proportionately less in moving around and staying alive.

Being gigantic is also a useful defense against predators once an animal has safely come through its early years and reached adult size. This explains why a number of

△ *American scientist Robert Bakker stands behind an* Apatosaurus *femur. Sauropod femurs are the largest single dinosaur bones.*

These sauropod bones are part of an immense collection at Dinosaur National Monument, on the border of Colorado and Utah. Giant leg bones, like the ones shown in the foreground, have been used to estimate the weight of the heaviest dinosaurs, including plant eaters and their predators. These estimates are made by measuring the bones' cross-sectional area at their narrowest point.

plant eaters, from horses to elephants, have grown larger during their evolutionary history. Unfortunately (from a plant eater's point of view), predators can also increase in size. During the dinosaur age the trend toward increasing size in plant eaters was mirrored by a similar trend in carnivores. This meant natural selection favored even larger plant eaters, and the process went on.

REACHING THE TOP

The bigger-is-better trend could not continue indefinitely, because the problems of being gigantic eventually started to outweigh the benefits. One of these problems was the difficulty of pumping blood to a head that towered many feet above the ground. *Brachiosaurus* and other long-necked sauropods would have needed powerful hearts, even if they did have tiny brains. Animals like these would also have faced increasing difficulties mating and laying eggs—a major consideration because producing plenty of young is the key to evolutionary success. But from an engineering standpoint a more fundamental problem concerned their weight: as they evolved larger and larger bodies, this climbed at a prodigious rate.

To visualize how this happened, imagine three dinosaurs shaped like cubes with sides 3 ft. (1m), 15 ft. (5m), and 30 ft. (10m) long. The second dinosaur is only five times as long as the first, but its weight is 125 times as great (the result of multiplying 5x5x5). The third dinosaur is 10 times as long, which means that it weighs a thousand times as much as the first. Once sauropods reached lengths of about 60 ft. (20m), each additional three feet meant a jump in weight of over a ton—a tremendous burden that still had to be supported by just four legs.

The strength of a leg depends on its cross-sectional area, rather than its volume. This means that if an animal gets larger but keeps the same overall shape, its weight outstrips its strength, so its legs are put under greater and greater stress. Sauropods coped with this by modifying their leg bones and by keeping bending to a minimum, but in the end it would have been weight, rather than anything else, that brought their growth to a halt.

WEIGHING A DINOSAUR
Leg dimensions are a useful way of weighing sauropods, even though these animals have been dead for millions of years. By measuring the cross-sectional area of a major leg bone, paleontologists can calculate the total weight of the living animal. Another method consists of making scale models: the model's volume is measured by putting it in water, and this figure is scaled up to calculate the final weight. But neither of these methods is 100 percent reliable. As a result the true weight of the world's heaviest dinosaurs will probably never be known.

▷ *Seen next to a* Brachiosaurus, Troodon *looks in danger of being squashed.* Brachiosaurus *may have weighed up to 80 tons—about 2,500 times as much as* Troodon *and about 80,000 times as much as* Saltopus, *the smallest dinosaur known.*

FOSSIL HUNTING IN SOUTH AMERICA

SOUTH AMERICA HAS PRODUCED SOME OF THE EARLIEST FOSSIL DINOSAURS, AND ALSO THE LARGEST, AS WELL AS SOME REMARKABLE EXTINCT MAMMALS AND BIRDS FROM MORE RECENT TIMES.

The geological history of South America makes it a fascinating place. Until the middle of the Mesozoic Era it was part of the great southern continent, Gondwana, which means that it shared many of the dinosaur families found in today's Africa and India. After the dinosaurs died out South America became an island, before joining with North America in much more recent times.

▽ *Rodolfo Coria—the scientist who unearthed* Argentiosaurus—*rests on one of the dinosaur's enormous spinal vertebrae.*

IN PATAGONIA

Over 160 years ago the renowned English naturalist Charles Darwin visited South America during his historic voyage on HMS *Beagle*. On this around-the-world expedition, he found fossils of extinct mammals such as the giant ground sloth *Megatherium*—an animal almost as large as an elephant—which was buried in gravel near the shore. The first fossil *Megatherium* had been seen by European scientists 50 years before, but for Darwin the process of uncovering its remains was momentous. It helped him appreciate the fact that extinction was a natural process—something that contributed to his theory of evolution.

Paleontologists still comb the

This fossilized skull, found in Ischigualasto National Park, Argentina, belonged to one of the earliest known dinosaurs, Eoraptor, a bipedal hunter just 3.3 ft. (1m) long. Although it lived over 200 million years ago, several almost complete skeletons have been found. In outward appearance, this small reptile was remarkably similar to some predatory dinosaurs that lived 100 million years later.

bleak Patagonian coastline, collecting fossils from the crumbling sedimentary rocks. But some of the most important discoveries have been found much farther inland, along the foothills that separate Argentina from neighboring Chile. This is South America's dinosaur country—a dry and dramatic part of the world where much older rocks bring a wealth of remains to the surface.

THE HUNT FOR EARLY DINOSAURS

From the late 1950s onward the moonlike surroundings of Argentina's Ischigualasto National Park have been the scene of some major dinosaur discoveries. In 1958 a local farmer found the first fragments of a small, meat-eating animal that lived during the late Triassic, making it the earliest dinosaur then known. Named *Herrerasaurus*, it shed new light on how dinosaurs might have originated from carnivorous reptiles (page 64). In 1988 American paleontologist Paul Sereno found further remains—a complete *Herrerasaurus* skull and several partial skeletons. In 1991 he identified the remains of an even older animal, called *Eoraptor*, which provided clues to how dinosaurs might have evolved.

Since South America was part of Gondwana when these animals were alive, it is unlikely that they lived only in this part of the world. But bare ground makes fossil hunting easier, which is why Ischigualasto is one of South America's foremost fossil hunting sites.

SOUTHERN GIANTS

South America is well known as a source of fossil sauropods—particularly titanosaurs, which were widespread in the southern continents. The list of species discovered in Argentina reads almost like a road map, because many of them, such as *Saltasaurus* and *Neuquensaurus*, take their names from the provinces where their fossil remains were found. But pride of place among these giants goes to *Argentinosaurus*, an animal named by two leading paleontologists, José F. Bonaparte and Rodolfo Coria, in 1993. *Argentinosaurus* may prove to be the world's largest dinosaur, although in North America there are several other contenders.

Rodolfo Coria also identified a giant predator, *Giganotosaurus*, whose remains were spotted in 1994 by an amateur fossil hunter in the foothills of the Andes. Weighing up to 8 tons, this tyrannosaur look-alike might have been the world's largest carnivorous dinosaur. Like *Argentinosaurus*, it lived throughout the Late Cretaceous, until the Age of Reptiles came to an end. So the world's largest plant eater and meat eater may have lived at the same time, and also in the same place—a double first!

FLYING GIANTS

In Argentina paleontologists have also found the remains of some enormous birds. Several of these were flightless, but one, *Argentavis magnificens*, may well have been the largest ever to have existed. Discovered in 1979 in the dusty pampas west of Buenos Aires, this animal had a wingspan of about 24.6 ft. (7.5m), which is more than twice the size of the largest flying birds today. *Argentavis* lived about 6 million years ago, and it belonged to a group of vulturelike birds called the teratorns, which later became extinct. It probably hunted living prey, using its large, hooked beak to make its kills. So did the phorusrhacoids, or terror birds—a line of flightless South American predators that stood up to 10 ft. (3m) high. Fossils suggest that these fearsome animals ran down their prey before using their beaks to rip it apart. Remains of over two dozen species have been found, but as with the teratorns, the entire group eventually disappeared.

◁ *In the far west of Argentina the stark landscape of Ischigualasto National Park, with its strangely sculpted cliffs and plateaus, is a magnet for paleontologists. Conditions can be tough: in the summer the heat is stifling, and the layers of pale claylike rock give off an intense glare in the bright sunshine.*

△ *A team of excavators including Rodolfo Coria (center) works at the Plaza Huincul site in Argentina, uncovering the enormous fossil bones of* Argentinosaurus huinculensis.

◁ *Unlike earlier reptiles,* Eoraptor *had fused vertebrae in its hip region. This gave it the extra structural strength needed to maintain an upright posture, with just two legs in contact with the ground.*

PLANT-EATING GIANTS

TITANOSAURS

Titanosaurs were the last sauropods to evolve, appearing in the Late Jurassic and surviving some 80 million years until the end of the Cretaceous. They were found across most of the world, but they were most widespread in the ancient southern continent of Gondwana. South America—which formed part of Gondwana—is where most of their remains have been discovered. They bore some resemblance to diplodocids, but were unique among sauropods in having bony armor, which consisted of hard plates scattered over their backs. Their other claim to fame is that a few grew to a truly incredible size. Remains of one as yet unclassified sauropod were found in southern Patagonia in 1999. The fossils included two vertebrae measuring 4 ft. (1.2m) in height and a thighbone 6 ft. (1.8m) long!

▽ *A titan among titans,* Argentinosaurus *may have been the largest dinosaur ever to have walked the earth—even if at a slow pace. As an adult this gigantic animal probably would have been immune from attack by most predators, but its young would still have been vulnerable. Here an adult is shown without armor-plating—whether it had plates is not known.*

ARGENTINOSAURUS
Argentina has produced some exciting fossil finds in recent years, and many paleontologists believe that this species— named in 1993—may turn out to be the largest dinosaur ever, although not the longest. So far only a few vertebrae and limb bones have been found, but they are built on an awe-inspiring scale. The biggest of the vertebrae measures 5 ft. (1.5m) in height, with a load-bearing center the size of a small tree. Scaling up from remains like these, experts estimate that the complete animal may have weighed in the range of 80 to 100 tons. Like other titanosaurs, *Argentinosaurus* had some unusual anatomical features not found in other sauropods. It had an extra vertebra in its sacrum—the part of the backbone that joins to the pelvic girdle. If it was like its relatives, its tail vertebrae would have been linked together with ball-and-socket joints. No traces of armor plating have actually been found, but as these plates are often scattered after death, it is still possible that *Argentinosaurus* shared this common family feature. With so little fossil evidence it is hard to say how this immense animal lived, although given its size, it would probably have needed to eat several tons of food a day.

MAXIMUM LENGTH 100 ft. (30m)
TIME Late Cretaceous
FOSSIL FINDS South America (Argentina)

ANTARCTOSAURUS
Despite its name, remains of this dinosaur have not been found in the Antarctic, but they have been discovered in South America and India, which once formed part of the great southern continent of Gondwana. None of these fossils is complete, but—unusually for a titanosaur—they include parts of the skull. From these finds *Antarctosaurus* seems to have been one of the largest and most widespread dinosaurs in the Southern Hemisphere. It had a square-ended lower jaw and small teeth, but so far no traces of armor-plating have been unearthed. In South America fossilized eggs have been found that are likely to have belonged either to this species, or to other members of the titanosaur family. About the size of small melons, some of them contain the fossilized embryos complete with impressions of skin.

MAXIMUM LENGTH 59 ft. (18m)
TIME Late Cretaceous
FOSSIL FINDS South America (Argentina, Brazil, Chile, Uruguay), Asia (India)

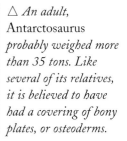
△ *An adult,* Antarctosaurus *probably weighed more than 35 tons. Like several of its relatives, it is believed to have had a covering of bony plates, or osteoderms.*

SALTASAURUS

Saltasaurus was officially named in 1980 after the province in Argentina where it was found. Compared to *Argentinosaurus*, it was a relatively small animal, with a back not much higher than an elephant's, although with a much longer and heavier body overall. Several fossilized skeletons have been found with thousands of small, bony plates lying around them, leading paleontologists to conclude that these plates would have covered the skin like armor. Some of the plates are no larger than peas and are attached to small relics of skin.

Others are about the size of a human hand and may have had a defensive spike. This discovery solved a long-running puzzle, because scattered plates have been uncovered before *Saltasaurus* fossils were found. Some scientists thought they belonged to nodosaurs (page 164), a group of unrelated dinosaurs that used armor for protection. *Saltasaurus* had robust limbs and a flexible tail, which may have helped it sit upright to feed. Remains of *Antarctosaurus* and *Argyrosaurus* have been found close to *Saltasaurus* fossils, raising the possibility that they, too, would have had armor-plated skin.

MAXIMUM LENGTH 40 ft. (12m)

TIME Late Cretaceous

FOSSIL FINDS South America (Argentina, Uruguay)

△ Saltasaurus *(center right), with its bony body armor, which would have protected it from predators, was a compact and stocky titanosaur with a small head and blunt teeth.*

NEUQUENSAURUS

Named after a town in Patagonia, this dinosaur closely resembled *Saltasaurus*, with a relatively small body covered in bony plates. The evidence for this comes from several fossil finds, including vertebrae, limb bones, and plates that were found in 1997. The similarities between the two dinosaurs seem to be very strong, and it is possible that future finds may show that they were actually the same dinosaur.

MAXIMUM LENGTH 50 ft. (15m)

TIME Late Cretaceous

FOSSIL FINDS South America (Argentina)

ARGYROSAURUS

The first remains of *Argyrosaurus* were discovered in the late 1800s. Its name means "silver lizard"—a reference to Argentina, or the "land of silver," which is where its fossils have been found. A massive animal, weighing as much as 80 tons, *Argyrosaurus* is known from only a few body parts, including the legs and some vertebrae. Paleontologists do not agree about where this animal fits into the titanosaur family— some think that the fossils may actually belong to *Antarctosaurus*.

MAXIMUM LENGTH 59 ft. (18m)

TIME Late Cretaceous

FOSSIL FINDS South America (Argentina)

HYPSELOSAURUS

Hypselosaurus was a relatively compact European titanosaur first identified from fossils in southern France nearly 150 years ago. The fossils were missing their skulls, but alongside them were several dozen basketball-sized eggs. These eggs were almost certainly laid by a *Hypselosaurus* and, at about 1 ft. (30cm) long, they are some of the largest dinosaur eggs currently known. Sauropods probably squatted down when they were ready to lay their eggs, but they may also have had an egg-laying tube that allowed the eggs to slide gently down to the ground.

MAXIMUM LENGTH 40 ft. (12m)

TIME Late Cretaceous

FOSSIL FINDS Europe (France, Spain)

PLANT-EATING GIANTS

MALAWISAURUS

Originally known as *Gigantosaurus*—
a name easily confused with *Giganotosaurus*
(page 143), a meat-eating allosaur—
Malawisaurus, is the oldest-known titanosaur
from Africa, dating back over 100 million
years. Relatively small by titanosaur standards,
it may have been armor-plated, but fossilized
plates have yet to be found. However, some
Malawisaurus fossils do include parts of the
animal's skull—rare for a titanosaur and for
sauropods as a whole. Titanosaur remains
have been found recently in nearby
Madagascar. Fortunately, these fossilized
remains also include parts of the skull.

MAXIMUM LENGTH	33 ft. **(10m)**
TIME	Early Cretaceous
FOSSIL FINDS	Africa (Malawi)

TITANOSAURUS

The most widespread member of its family,
Titanosaurus was first discovered in 1877
in India. The original fossil consisted of a
broken thighbone and some tail vertebrae,
but since then further finds have been
made in many places around the world,
including Madagascar. The Indian find
was particularly important, because it was
the first major dinosaur discovery in what
was once part of Gondwana, although
continental drift was not known about at
the time. Some paleontologists think that
Titanosaurus had armor-plating, but there
is not strong enough evidence of this.

MAXIMUM LENGTH	65.6 ft. (20m)
TIME	Late Cretaceous
FOSSIL FINDS	South America (Argentina), Europe (France), Asia (India), Africa (Madagascar)

ALAMOSAURUS

Alamosaurus is the only titanosaur found
in North America. It was also one of the
last sauropods, surviving until the end of
the Cretaceous Period when it—and all
other dinosaurs—died out. Found in the
western United States, its remains are more
complete than those of most of its relatives,
although they are missing the skull.

Alamosaurus weighed about 30 tons,
and had a long, whip-ended tail. Unlike
many other titanosaurs, it seems to have
had no body armor. Even when it was
alive, *Alamosaurus* would have looked like
a relic from the past, because by the Late
Cretaceous Period sauropods were no longer
the dominant plant eaters and had dwindled
to a fraction of the importance they had
had in Jurassic times. *Alamosaurus'* status as
North America's sole titanosaur is probably
explained by geological changes. For
millions of years North and South America
were separated by sea, but during the Late
Cretaceous temporary land bridges linked
the two continents. *Alamosaurus*—or its
ancestors—took this opportunity to head
north, but its history was cut short when
the Age of Dinosaurs came to an end.

MAXIMUM LENGTH	69 ft. (21m)
TIME	Late Cretaceous
FOSSIL FINDS	North America (Montana, New Mexico, Texas, Utah)

▽ Alamosaurus *lived
in North America in
the dying days of the
dinosaurs. It was named
after the Ojo Alamo
trading post in New
Mexico, where a set
of its remains
was found.*

ORNITHOPODS

The ornithopods were a group of ornithischian, or bird-hipped, plant eaters that first appeared early in the Jurassic, about 200 million years ago. They included the iguanodonts—some of the first dinosaurs to be discovered—as well as the hadrosaurs, a remarkable family of reptiles often adorned with bizarre crests. Together with the fabrosaurs, heterodontosaurs, and hypsilophodonts, these animals included some of the most successful and numerous plant eaters during the Cretaceous. Ornithopods never equaled sauropods in size, but they were abundant when sauropods themselves were in decline.

DANGER ON THE HORIZON

Making their daily visit to a sandy riverbed, a mixed group of hadrosaurs—including mothers with their young—pause to drink and rest in the morning sunshine. But this tranquil scene is not destined to last. A tyrannosaur has appeared on a distant sandbank, and some of the adult hadrosaurs are getting ready to run. The hadrosaurs could call to each other using their hollow crests, to warn of the impending danger. (See key on page 94.)

LIFE IN A GROUP

FOR PLANT-EATING DINOSAURS, LIVING IN HERDS WAS A VITAL SURVIVAL TECHNIQUE IN A WORLD FULL OF DANGEROUS PREDATORS.

Millions of years after the dinosaurs died out, there is still plenty of evidence showing that some of them lived in herds. This includes fossilized mass graves, where entire herds were overtaken by disasters such as sandstorms, as well as communal nesting sites and sets of tracks left by herds on the move.

HERD SIZES

How large were dinosaur herds? Fossilized bones and tracks provide the best clues, but they have to be interpreted with care. Animals can be at the same place at the same time without forming a herd. This often happens at waterholes, when animals that normally live on their own gather to drink. Collections of bones can also be misleading, because they may belong to animals that died weeks or even years apart. This can happen when they are the victims of the same hazard—a slippery slope— or when hunters use a favorite spot for attacking their prey.

Paleontologists have examined many sets of fossils and come up with a variety of figures for different species. There are records of iguanodonts traveling in groups of four or five; hadrosaurs such as *Maiasaura* seem to have lived in herds of several hundred, scattered over a wide area.

DINOSAUR SOCIAL LIFE

Herd-forming species almost certainly showed complex forms of behavior. As with today's herding mammals, animals of different ages and sexes would have had different statuses, and often a different position in the herd. Some fossilized tracks back up this idea, because the smallest prints —belonging to young animals—are often found in the center, and those left by the largest adults are at the front and around the sides. This would have protected the young

and allowed the adults to form
a barrier if a predator did try to attack.

JOINING AND LEAVING

Animals grow up and die, so the makeup
of a herd changes all the time. But herds
can change in other ways. In many of today's
herding animals, such as elephants, males
leave the herd once they can look after
themselves and live in bachelor herds for
several years. The strongest adult males then
head herds of their own, which include several
females and young. It is likely that some
dinosaurs had similar social systems. During
their time in bachelor herds the males would
have engaged in mock fights with their rivals.
This kind of fighting is unlikely to have
caused permanent injuries, but it would have
separated out the strongest and fittest males,
allowing them to father the most young.

INDIVIDUAL RECOGNITION

Dinosaur fossils often show variations
between members of the same species. The
most obvious differences are between males
and females, but there are also differences
between one individual and another. These
small variations may have worked like
identity badges, helping herd members
identify each other. Because dinosaurs were
often long-lived, older animals could have
decades of experience in recognizing the
other members of their herd. Each animal
would have known where it fit in the herd's
pecking order and where its place was
if the herd came under attack.

▽ *Threatened by a pair
of tyrannosaurs, adult*
Centrosaurus *form a
defensive ring around
their young. In this kind
of emergency the young
animals would have
instinctively rushed for the
middle of the ring, while
the adults turned their
horns on the aggressors.
The disadvantage of
the ring defense was
that the entire herd
was effectively trapped—
until the predators either
abandoned their attack
or made a kill.*

ORNITHOPODS

HYPSILOPHODONTS

The hypsilophodonts were the dinosaur world's equivalent of horses and antelopes, living in large herds, and feeding on low growing plants. Like other ornithopods, they had a short, beaklike muzzle, muscular cheeks, and well-developed chewing teeth. Their cheeks were an important step forward, because they helped them hold their food in place to chew. Hypsilophodonts were fairly small animals, but during their 100-million-year history they became widespread and were eventually found on almost every continent, including Australia.

▽ Hypsilophodon (left) gets its name from its tall, ridged cheek teeth. The upper and lower sets met to form a perfect grinding surface, and they were self-sharpening—features that were shared by all members of the family. Dryosaurus (right) used its beak to tear up mouthfuls of vegetation. While it was chewing it would probably have raised its head so that it could watch for danger—a kind of behavior seen in most of today's plant eaters that live in open habitats.

DRYOSAURUS

Dryosaurus was a medium-sized member of the family and one of the earliest to evolve. Its body was supported by a pair of sturdy legs, with a stiff, heavy tail that acted as a counterbalance for its head and neck and its large plant eater's stomach. Its muzzle ended in a hard-edged beak, which could tear off plants close to the ground. Like other ornithopods, it had few defenses, and it is likely to have been an effective middle-distance runner. Unusually for a hypsilophodont, its feet had only three toes.

MAXIMUM LENGTH 13 ft. (4m)

TIME Late Jurassic

FOSSIL FINDS Africa (Tanzania), North America (Colorado, Wyoming)

HYPSILOPHODON

Less than 3.3 ft. (1m) tall and with a head no larger than a human hand, *Hypsilophodon* is known from some superbly preserved fossils. They include a group of about two dozen animals discovered on England's Isle of Wight, which may have been members of a small herd trapped by a rising tide. These fossils show that it had five-fingered hands and four-toed feet, and perhaps a double row of bony plates running down its back. During the 1800s, when *Hypsilophodon* was first discovered, British zoologist Thomas Huxley suggested it was shaped for climbing and might have lived in trees like today's tree kangaroo. Paleontologists now think that it is likely to have lived on the ground.

MAXIMUM LENGTH 7.5 ft. (2.3m)

TIME Early Cretaceous

FOSSIL FINDS Europe (Portugal, Spain, U.K.), North America (South Dakota)

LEAELLYNASAURA

Studies of this Australian hypsilophodont have provided support for the idea that some dinosaurs were warm-blooded (page 148). Its fossilized remains were found at a site on the Southern coast of Australia, known as Dinosaur Cove, well within the Antarctic Circle when *Leaellynasaura* was alive. Although the climate was significantly

FULGUROTHERIUM

This dinosaur was named after Lightning Ridge in New South Wales, Australia, a well-known opal mining area and dinosaur fossil site where incomplete remains—a skull, a thighbone, and teeth—were found in 1932.

MAXIMUM LENGTH	6.6 ft. (2m)
TIME	Early Cretaceous
FOSSIL FINDS	Australia (New South Wales)

△ *Weighing as little as 22 lbs. (10kg), Leaellynasaura (left) was about the size of an ostrich. If it was warm-blooded, it may have had featherlike insulation. It lived in herds, feeding on cycads, ferns, and conifers. Fulgurotherium (right) also lived during the Cretaceous, when Australia was one of the coldest parts of the southern continent Gondwana.*

warmer then, life this far south would still have been a challenge—particularly in the winter, when daylight and food were in short supply. If *Leaellynasaura* was warm-blooded rather than cold-blooded, it could have remained active all year round. There is no physical evidence for this, but *Leaellynasaura* did have enlarged eye sockets and a large brain, which means that it would have been good at finding its way in the dim winter light. *Leaellynasaura* was discovered in 1989, and named after the daughters of the two paleontologists who found it.

MAXIMUM LENGTH	9.8 ft. (3m)
TIME	Mid Cretaceous
FOSSIL FINDS	Australia (Victoria)

TENONTOSAURUS

Tenontosaurus was exceptionally large for a hypsilophodont, and this, with details of its skull anatomy, make some paleontologists think that it may have been an iguanodont. Its teeth, however, are of the typical hypsilophodont type—an important point, because it is rare for identical tooth types to evolve twice. Like other ornithopods, *Tenontosaurus* probably dropped onto all fours when feeding, and, because it weighed over a ton, it may have rested like this as well.

MAXIMUM LENGTH	23 ft. (7m)
TIME	Early Cretaceous
FOSSIL FINDS	North America (Arizona, Montana, Oklahoma, Texas)

ORNITHOPODS

FABROSAURS

Small and lightly built, the fabrosaurs were the reptilian equivalent of hare or small deer, using their narrow mouths to pick out nutritious vegetation on or close to the ground. They walked and ran only on their back legs, using their long tails for balance. Most of them were less than 6.6 ft. (2m) long, and unlike many other plant eaters, they may have foraged alone. Fabrosaurs were among the earliest ornithopods to evolve. Some paleontologists actually consider them to be a parallel group, because they did not have the features shared by ornithopods as a whole.

▽ *Although not tough enough to deter large predators*, Scutellosaurus' *body armor would have made it a tricky target for a hunter nearer its own size. Body armor was an unusual feature in dinosaurs this small.*

▽ *From the neck down* Lesothosaurus *looked similar to some of the smaller theropods, but its shorter jaws showed that it was a plant eater, not a hunter.*

LESOTHOSAURUS
Only a handful of *Lesothosaurus* fossils are known. But one set is very interesting, because it shows a pair of animals huddled together, possibly in a burrow underground. *Lesothosaurus* lived in a hot, dry habitat, and the likeliest explanation for this huddle is that the two animals were estivating—a summer equivalent of hibernation. By becoming dormant, they would have saved energy at a time of year when plant food was difficult to find. Physically *Lesothosaurus* looked like some small predatory dinosaurs, but its pointed teeth were shaped for dealing with plants. It had long leg bones, and its defense against predators would have been to run away.

MAXIMUM LENGTH	3.3 ft. (1m)
TIME	Early Jurassic
FOSSIL FINDS	Africa (Lesotho)

▷ Echindon *is sometimes classified as a heterodontosaur, because it shared their pattern of varied teeth. As a small plant eater it could not process large quantities of food, and it probably survived by being selective about what it ate. Its narrow snout was ideal for this way of life*

SCUTELLOSAURUS
This fabrosaur's name means "little shield lizard." It is the only fabrosaur known to have had body armor, consisting of small bony plates down its neck and back. This coat of armor brought practical problems— mainly extra weight. *Scutellosaurus* may have spent some of its time on all fours, to spread the load. However, even with its armor, it probably weighed only about 22 lb. (10kg).

MAXIMUM LENGTH	4 ft. (1.2m)
TIME	Early Jurassic
FOSSIL FINDS	North America (Arizona)

ECHINDON
Echindon was a tiny plant eater, weighing not much more than a large domestic cat. It had a small head and narrow snout, with two types of teeth. It probably nipped off nutritious new plant growth, leaving tougher leaves for other animals.

MAXIMUM LENGTH	2 ft. (60cm)
TIME	Late Jurassic
FOSSIL FINDS	Europe (England)

HETERODONTOSAURS

Dinosaurs sometimes had a lot of teeth, but as a rule, each kind of dinosaur had only a single type. Heterodontosaurs were different because they had teeth that were specifically shaped for carrying out different tasks. This kind of specialized dentition is common in mammals, including humans, but in reptiles it was—and still is— highly unusual. Heterodontosaurs walked on their hind legs, and they relied on speed to escape from their enemies.

HETERODONTOSAURUS

When *Heterodontosaurus* was discovered in the 1960s, it quickly became clear that it was an early ornithopod with some remarkable features. It had three types of teeth. These included sharp cutting teeth at the front of its upper jaw, which bit down onto a toothless lower beak; and cheek teeth, which ground up its food. It also had two pairs of extra-long teeth, or tusks, that resembled a mammal's stabbing canines—strange for an animal that clearly fed on plants. The most widely accepted explanation is that *Heterodontosaurus* used the tusks for fighting rivals. A very similar animal called *Abrictosaurus* did not have tusks, and many experts think this is actually a female *Heterodontosaurus* that has been classified by mistake. An adult, *Heterodontosaurus* stood about 19.7 in. (50cm) high and probably weighed less than 44 lb. (20kg).

MAXIMUM LENGTH	4 ft. (1.2m)
TIME	Early Jurassic
FOSSIL FINDS	Africa (South Africa)

LYCORHINUS

Like *Heterodontosaurus*, this small plant eater also lived in southern Africa, but so far only its lower jaw has been discovered. It was thought to belong to a mammal, because it had specialized teeth, including two tusks. However, a closer look showed that the animal's lower jaw was made of several bones rather than one— a sign that it was actually a reptile. Judging from its jaw, *Lycorhinus* was similar in size to *Heterodontosaurus* and would also have been a grazer, feeding on low-growing plants.

MAXIMUM LENGTH	4 ft. (1.2m)
TIME	Early Jurassic
FOSSIL FINDS	Africa (South Africa)

PISANOSAURUS

Uncertainty surrounds this small South American plant eater which was discovered in the 1960s. From its fragmentary remains, some paleontologists have concluded that it was an ornithopod, perhaps belonging to the heterodontosaur line. If true, this would make it one of the earliest ornithischians, or bird-hipped, dinosaurs (page 70). If they were heterodontosaurs, this family provides evidence that Africa and South America were joined together in Triassic times.

MAXIMUM LENGTH	3.3 ft. (1m)
TIME	Late Triassic
FOSSIL FINDS	South America (Argentina)

△ *The name* Heterodontosaurus *means "different teeth." The animal in this reconstruction has large canines, which may have been a feature found only in males. The front of the lower jaw was toothless, and the upper jaw had teeth— an interesting reversal of the jaw structure found in today's grazing mammals.*

◁ Pisanosaurus *was discovered in the same rock formation as* Herrerasaurus *and* Eoraptor, *two other very early dinosaurs from South America. However, unlike these animals, it was a plant eater, although it still retained the primitive feature of walking on two legs.*

ORNITHOPODS

IGUANODONTS

Iguanodonts were among the first dinosaurs to be discovered and identified, nearly 200 years ago. They were probably descended from the hypsilophodonts, but they got their name because their teeth resembled those of present-day iguanas. Iguanodonts were large, relatively slow-moving plant eaters. Their back legs were larger than their front legs, and they could probably move on either four legs or two. Most species had sharply pointed thumbs.

▷ *Iguanodonts may have used their spikelike thumbs as defensive weapons. Here an* Iguanodon *fends off a predatory theropod.*

▽ *Many iguanodonts had dextrous front feet, with four fingers as well as a sharp thumb. The three middle fingers were hooflike. The fourth was much smaller and could fold across the palm. It allowed them to pick up food.*

IGUANODON
Easily the largest member of its family, *Iguanodon* stood three times the height of a man and weighed 4.5 tons. It is one of the most famous dinosaurs, because it was discovered by Mary Mantell in 1822, when dinosaurs were still unknown to science. The English geologist who described it—Mary's husband, Gideon Mantell—realized that it was a giant reptile, but mistakenly thought that its thumb spikes were horns. *Iguanodon* was a highly successful plant eater with a long skull, beaklike jaws, and rows of grinding cheek teeth that help to distinguish ornithopods from other herbivorous dinosaurs.
It lived on all the continents except for Antarctica. In some fossil sites—for example, in Belgium—the remains of many iguanodons have been found side by side, suggesting that they lived in herds.

MAXIMUM LENGTH	30 ft. (9m)
TIME	Early Cretaceous
FOSSIL FINDS	Europe, North Africa, Asia (Mongolia), North America

CALLOVOSAURUS
Little is known about *Callovosaurus*, because the only fossil remains are of a single thighbone, which was discovered in England. However, the rocks surrounding this fossil show that this is the earliest iguanodont that has been found so far.
It was probably similar in general appearance to *Camptosaurus*, although little more than half its length.

MAXIMUM LENGTH	11.5 ft (3.5m)
TIME	Middle Jurassic
FOSSIL FINDS	Europe (England)

CAMPTOSAURUS
Another early iguanodont, *Camptosaurus* was common in North America and Europe about 150 million years ago, where it most likely lived in herds. It was a heavy-boned creature, weighing over one ton, with much shorter arms than legs, and a long skull that ended in a toothless beak. Its teeth were at the rear of its mouth—the ideal place for producing the force needed to crush plant food. While earlier plant eaters had to pause to breathe *Camptosaurus* had a long bony palate attached to the roof of its mouth, allowing it to breathe and eat simultaneously. Unlike *Iguanodon*, its wrists were not well developed, which suggests that it walked on its back legs, rather than on all fours.

MAXIMUM LENGTH	23 ft. (7m)
TIME	Late Jurassic
FOSSIL FINDS	Western North America, Europe (England, Portugal)

VECTISAURUS
Vectisaurus—named after the Latin for the Isle of Wight in England—was a close relative of *Iguanodon* and lived at the same time. It differed only in its smaller size and

IGUANODONTS

in having a spiny ridge running along its backbone. Paleontologists are unsure what part this ridge played in the animal's daily life. It may have been used to regulate body temperature, but its small size makes that doubtful.

MAXIMUM LENGTH 13 ft. (4m)
TIME Early Cretaceous
FOSSIL FINDS Europe (England)

OURANOSAURUS

Like *Vectisaurus*, this animal also had a spiny ridge along its back, but it was much more pronounced, forming a fan-shaped structure up to 20 in. (50cm) high. The ridge ran from the shoulders and extended halfway down the tail. *Ouranosaurus* also had an unusual head for an iguanodont, with a flat top, a raised bony brow above the eyes, and a snout leading to a wide, beaklike mouth.

MAXIMUM LENGTH 23 ft. (7m)
TIME Early Cretaceous
FOSSIL FINDS West Africa

MUTTABURRASAURUS

Named after a small town in Queensland, Australia, *Muttaburrasaurus* is believed to have been another close relative of *Iguanodon*. It was similar, although smaller, with some telltale differences in the structure of its head. One of these was a characteristic bony lump on its nose, which may have been used in courtship displays. Another was a pair of unusually large nostrils, suggesting that it had a good sense of smell to find food. *Muttaburrasaurus* also had teeth shaped for cutting rather than grinding, which may mean that it was at least partly carnivorous. Like most other iguanodonts, it had large spikelike thumbs.

MAXIMUM LENGTH 7m (23 ft.)
TIME Early Cretaceous
FOSSIL FINDS Australia

◁ *The first remains of* Muttaburrasaurus *were discovered in 1963. This iguanodont lived at a time when Australia was slowly separating from the southern continents, carrying dinosaurs and other animals with it. Even today little is known about Australia's dinosaurs.*

▽ Ouranosaurus *herds once roamed what is now West Africa, eating plants in the hot and sometimes swampy landscape. The fan-shaped skin on their backs may have helped with heat regulation. By turning the fan to face the sun, they could have absorbed heat.*

101

COLORS AND CAMOUFLAGE

AT ONE TIME DINOSAURS WERE THOUGHT TO BE UNIFORMLY DRAB AND GRAY. HOWEVER, TODAY'S EXPERTS BELIEVE THAT THE DINOSAUR WORLD MAY HAVE BEEN A SURPRISINGLY COLORFUL PLACE.

Fossils reveal a great deal about the internal structure of dinosaurs, but they very rarely include any sign of their skin. This is because, like most other soft parts of the body, skin usually breaks down before fossils are formed. Occasionally some traces of the skin texture are left, and these show that dinosaurs were often covered with pebblelike nodules or sometimes lizardlike scales. But so far no clear evidence of skin pigmentation has been found. Without this, paleontologists have to rely on studies of living animals to picture what dinosaurs may have looked like.

HIDING AWAY
The colors and patterns of dinosaurs almost certainly depended on how they lived. Giant plant eaters, such as the brachiosaurs and titanosaurs, had relatively few enemies when they were fully grown, so they had very little need to hide away. Added to this, their huge size meant that they would have been almost impossible to conceal. As a result they probably had plain but muted colors—the kind of color schemes that all dinosaurs were once thought to have had and the ones that elephants and rhinos have today.

But with smaller planteaters, such as hadrosaurs, the situation was very different. These animals had many enemies, and one of their best defenses, apart from running away, was to avoid being seen. Over a long period of time evolution may well have given them camouflage as a form of self-protection. To see what they may have looked like, biologists turn to reptiles that live today. Plant-eating reptiles are now very rare, and most of them, such as iguanas, are brown or green.

CHANGING COLOR
Some of today's reptiles, most famously the chameleons, can change their color to mimic their background. It is very likely that some dinosaurs were also able to do this, because the few fossils that have been found show that their skin seems to have the same structure. But chameleons do not switch color only to hide, they also do it to show their mood. Unlike camouflage colors, these mood-indicating colors are often vivid, with contrasting streaks and stripes. As a form of communication they are difficult to miss.

FLUSHES AND BLUSHES

The variations in skin colors would have been produced by pigment-containing cells close to the surface of the skin. By altering the distribution of pigment in each cell, different color schemes could be produced. But there is another way that dinosaurs might have changed color—by altering the flow of blood. Many experts believe this could have happened in stegosaurs (pages 158–159), which had rows of bony plates extending down their backs. There are signs that these plates had a rich blood supply flowing through them and through a surface layer of skin. Stegosaurs may have used the plates to warm up or cool down, blushing as they increased their supply of blood.

These blushes might have served a double function, by also acting as a form of communication between the dinosaurs. It is not hard to imagine one blushing male *Stegosaurus* squaring up to another as the two prepare to fight.

SEX DIFFERENCES

In living reptiles males and females often look similar, but the same is not true of many birds. Because dinosaurs were the ancestors of birds, it is possible that they, too, showed marked color differences between the sexes. In some species, for example the bone-headed dinosaurs (pages 166–167), males and females differed in size, so they may have differed in color as well.

This remarkable fossil from Wyoming shows the knobbly skin of Edmontosaurus, a duck-billed dinosaur. The fossil was formed from a mummified corpse. The process of mummification hardens the skin, so it fossilizes along with the animal's bones. Traces of skin texture are sometimes preserved in dinosaurs that died on damp mud. The mud makes a mold of the skin, and this is preserved when the mud is fossilized.

▽ *These three reconstructions show imaginary color schemes for Parasaurolophus, a duck-billed dinosaur. Even though it grew to 33 ft. (10m) long, Parasaurolophus would have made a tempting target for tyrannosaurs, and camouflage would have been a useful first step toward avoiding attack. The green and brown pigments shown here are typical of those found in today's reptiles.*

103

ORNITHOPODS

HADROSAURS

Hadrosaurs are often known as duck-billed dinosaurs, because they had flattened, beaklike snouts. Some also sported hollow crests, which had a variety of eccentric shapes. These crests contained nasal tubes, and it is possible that they allowed hadrosaurs to make loud calls (see page 112). Hadrosaurs were herd-forming vegetarians, generally feeding on four legs, but able to run away on two. They were one of the last and most successful of the dinosaur families, originating in Asia and spreading to North America and Europe.

MAIASAURA

Many of the dinosaurs left few traces to show how they lived and bred, but with *Maiasaura* the evidence is astounding. Paleontologists have discovered this hadrosaur's nests and eggs and animals at almost every age, from hatchlings to adults. The females built nest mounds out of mud, and they may have covered their eggs with soil to keep them warm and hidden from hungry eyes. After the young hatched it is likely that the females cared for them until they were capable of fending for themselves. Fossils also show that *Maiasaura* lived in herds—possibly thousands

strong. *Maiasaura* had only a modest crest, but when fully grown it weighed up to four tons. Fossilized droppings indicate that it fed on tough, woody plants.

MAXIMUM LENGTH	30 ft. (9m)
TIME	Late Cretaceous
FOSSIL FINDS	North America

BACTROSAURUS

Bactrosaurus was probably one of the earliest hadrosaurs to evolve, and it had fewer teeth in its cheeks than later species. It was also one of the smallest, although still a substantial animal. It had a flat, uncrested head, and high spikes on its vertebrae produced a ridge down its back. Unlike larger hadrosaurs, it always walked on its hind legs.

MAXIMUM LENGTH	20 ft. (6m)
TIME	Late Cretaceous
FOSSIL FINDS	Asia (Mongolia, China)

HADROSAURUS

Hadrosaurus, which means "big lizard," was the first dinosaur to be discovered in the U.S.A., in 1858. The partial remains—which were missing the skull—were enough to show that this massive plant eater could stand on two legs. Since then many more fossils have been found, revealing that *Hadrosaurus* had a duck-billed head with a raised lump on its snout, but not a crest like some other members of its family. It also had a battery of grinding teeth at the back of its jaws. These were continuously replaced as they wore down, unlike the teeth of today's plant-eating mammals, which have to last for life. *Hadrosaurus* fed on a tough diet of leaves, branches, and seeds.

MAXIMUM LENGTH	33 ft. (10m)
TIME	Late Cretaceous
FOSSIL FINDS	North America (Alberta, Montana, New Jersey, New Mexico)

◁ *Standing by her nest mound, a female* Maiasaura *tends her newly hatched young.* Maiasaura *nests were up to 6.5 ft. (2m) across and held up to two dozen grapefruit-sized eggs.*

TSINTAOSAURUS

This Chinese hadrosaur has a particularly bizarre crest, consisting of a single horn nearly 3.3 ft. (1m) long, emerging from a point between the eyes. When the first fossilized skull was found the crest was thought to be an accidental result of preservation. However, further finds showing the same feature proved that this was not the case. The crest is usually shown as jutting forward, but no one knows exactly how it was really positioned. It may have been an isolated structure—making *Tsintaosaurus* look like the dinosaur equivalent of a unicorn—but it is also possible that it was connected to flaps of skin. Otherwise *Tsintaosaurus* seems to have had a typical hadrosaur build, with relatively small front legs but much larger hind ones.

MAXIMUM LENGTH 33 ft. (10m)

TIME Late Cretaceous

FOSSIL FINDS Asia (China)

CORYTHOSAURUS

Corythosaurus, meaning "helmet lizard," was a large hadrosaur with a dome-shaped crest. The crest was hollow, and it contained spaces that were connected to its nasal passages. The crest's size varied from one animal to another and was probably largest in mature males. This size difference makes it likely that the crest was used in courtship displays, but it may also have played a part in helping *Corythosaurus* keep cool. Fossilized impressions of this animal's skin show that it had a pebbly texture.

MAXIMUM LENGTH 30 ft. (9m)

TIME Late Cretaceous

FOSSIL FINDS North America (Alberta, Montana)

EDMONTOSAURUS

Hadrosaurs were the only dinosaurs that could chew their food because of their unusual teeth, which were arranged in several interlocking rows at the back of their jaws. *Edmontosaurus*—one of the largest of the family—had up to 1,000 teeth, which were brought together by powerful cheek muscles. Fossils of mummified animals show that *Edmontosaurus* had raised nodules on the surface of its skin, and many scientists think that it had loose skin around its nose. It may have been able to inflate this like a balloon, either as a mating ritual or as a warning to rivals. Like other hadrosaurs, its only real defense was to run away from danger on its back legs, although it may have been able to swim. Its size meant that it was not a sprinter, leaving it vulnerable to tyrannosaurs and other giant predators.

MAXIMUM LENGTH 43 ft. (13m)

TIME Late Cretaceous

FOSSIL FINDS North America (Alberta, Montana)

KRITOSAURUS

Very similar in size and appearance to *Hadrosaurus*, this crestless hadrosaur may have been one of its closest relatives. Like *Hadrosaurus*, it had a bony lump on its snout, making it look as if it had a broken nose. It probably weighed between two and three tons. Its remains were found in 1910 by Barnum Brown, a great collector from the American Museum of Natural History, in New York City.

MAXIMUM LENGTH 43 ft. (13m)

TIME Late Cretaceous

FOSSIL FINDS North America (Texas, New Mexico)

▽ *The hadrosaur family divided into two groups.* Tstintaosaurus *and* Corythosaurus *belonged to the lambeosaurine group, containing species with flamboyant crests.* Edmontosaurus *and* Kritosaurus *belonged to the hadrosaurine group— their crests were either small or nonexistent.*

Corythosaurus

Tsintaosaurus

Edmontosaurus

Kritosaurus

ORNITHOPODS

▷ *Fossils of*
Lambeosaurus
magnicristatus have
been found in Alberta,
and in Montana.
The animal's helmet-
shaped crest had a small,
backward-pointing spike,
but this was probably
covered by a flap of skin
that merged with the
neck. This illustration
shows an adult male.

LAMBEOSAURUS

Lambeosaurus is the largest duck-billed dinosaur discovered so far. One species, *Lambeosaurus lambei*, had a bizarre two-part crest (page 92) consisting of a backward-pointing spike and a forward-pointing part that looked like the blade of a hatchet emerging from between its eyes. Another species, *Lambeosaurus magnicristatus*, looked more like *Corythosaurus* (page 105), with a dome-shaped crest. At one time it was thought that *Lambeosaurus* and its relatives fed in water, using their tails as paddles, but most paleontologists are now convinced that they lived on land.

MAXIMUM LENGTH 50 ft. (15m)

TIME Late Cretaceous

FOSSIL FINDS North America

▷ *Saurolophus had*
a long, flattened head
ending in a hornlike
crest. Unusually, it
also had a ring of
bones around its eyes—
a feature common in
reptiles but absent from
many other members of
the hadrosaur family.
Its long "beak" was
toothless, but hundreds
of teeth were packed
together toward the rear
of the animal's jaws.

SAUROLOPHUS

Found in North America and Asia, *Saurolophus* had a solid bony crest, about 6 in. (15cm) long, on top of its head. Some paleontologists think that the crest may have been connected to a flap of skin that could be inflated with air. If this is true, *Saurolophus* could have used it to produce honking sounds, which would have carried a long distance to attract mates or warn the rest of the herd of danger. Many fossils have been found—the largest specimens come from Asia.

MAXIMUM LENGTH 40 ft. (12m)

TIME Late Cretaceous

FOSSIL FINDS North America, Asia (Mongolia)

▷ *Parasaurolophus'*
crest was the longest
of all the hadrosaurs'
crests. Males had larger
crests than females, giving
strength to the theory
that their elongated crests
were primarily used in
courtship, either through
their appearance or by
making sounds.

PARASAUROLOPHUS

With its extraordinary crest, this dinosaur was one of the most remarkable products of the dinosaur age. The crest was up to 6 ft. (1.8m) long, and it swept backward from the animal's head, ending in a bony knob. The nostrils were connected to the crest by hollow tubes, which ran all the way along the crest and then back down. At first sight this bizarre structure looks like a type of snorkel, but because it was not open-ended, it could not have worked in this way. Instead, it may have been used during courtship displays and could have produced calls as deep as a foghorn, which would have been audible many miles away. *Parasaurolophus* had well-developed front legs, suggesting that it spent most of its time on all fours.

MAXIMUM LENGTH 33 ft. (10m)

TIME Late Cretaceous

FOSSIL FINDS North America

ANATOSAURUS

A lot is known about *Anatosaurus* because some exceptionally well-preserved fossils have been found, as well as some mummified specimens that reveal details of skin and internal organs. Weighing over 3 tons, it was a classic duck-billed dinosaur, with a wide head ending in a beaklike mouth. (*Anatosaurus* means "duck lizard.") As in other hadrosaurs, its beak had no teeth. These were located farther back in its jaws. Stomach remains show that it ate pine needles, twigs, seeds, and fruit. It was once thought to be semiaquatic because some foot remains seem to show webbing between the toes. Experts have since concluded that these flaps of skin were the remains of pads that bore the animal's weight on land.

MAXIMUM LENGTH 43 ft. (13m)

TIME Late Cretaceous

FOSSIL FINDS North America

SHANTUNGOSAURUS

Shantungosaurus was one of the largest of the hadrosaurs and one of the largest plant-eating dinosaurs capable of walking on two legs. It weighed about 7 tons and when standing on its back legs would have been about 23 ft. (7m) tall. Half its length consisted of its huge tail, which would have acted as a counterbalance when it walked upright. This dinosaur did not have a crest, but it did have the beaklike mouth that is typical of its family, with teeth positioned at the back of the jaws. Even though it was a bird-hipped dinosaur, rather than a lizard-hipped sauropod, *Shantungosaurus* would have had almost as much effect on plant life as they did, because of its immense size. *Shantungosaurus* gets its name from Shandong province, in eastern China, where an almost complete skeleton was found in 1973.

MAXIMUM LENGTH 50 ft. (15m)

TIME Late Cretaceous

FOSSIL FINDS North America, Central Asia

▽ Hypacrosaurus *had a prominent, hollow crest, like some ground-dwelling birds have today. It would have been useful for pushing through vegetation, but its true function will probably never be known.*

HYPACROSAURUS

Like *Corythosaurus* (page 105), this dinosaur had a hollow, helmetlike crest, with an almost identical internal structure. It also had a ridged back and lived in herds, feeding on all fours. An insight into this dinosaur's family life has come from a nest of eight large fossilized eggs discovered in Alberta. The eggs were the size of melons and contained fossilized embryos. Arranged in rows, they were probably buried until they were ready to hatch. The eggs may have been covered with soil and vegetation—a mixture that would have produced heat as the plants rotted, helping the young dinosaurs develop.

Like *Maiasaura*, the parents probably guarded their nests.

MAXIMUM LENGTH 30 ft. (9m)

TIME Late Cretaceous

FOSSIL FINDS North America (Alberta, Montana)

FOSSIL HUNTING IN ASIA

STRETCHING ALMOST HALFWAY AROUND THE GLOBE, ASIA CONTAINS SOME OF THE BEST FOSSIL-HUNTING SITES IN THE WORLD. PALEONTOLOGISTS HAVE UNEARTHED A WEALTH OF SPECTACULAR FINDS.

Southern Asia has seen a number of important dinosaur discoveries, but perhaps the most interesting finds have been farther north, in Russia, Mongolia, and China. During the 1900s political problems meant access for western experts was limited, but this did not stop research. Russian scientists have built up the largest museum collections of fossils in the world, and in China recent discoveries have thrown new light on the evolution of birds.

With its giant jaws gaping wide, this fully assembled fossil of Tarbosaurus *gives a spine-chilling impression of Asia's largest land predator. The first remains of* Tarbosaurus *were found in the Gobi region in 1955, and since then about a dozen skeletons have been found. Some are almost complete and show the huge difference in size between the animal's back legs and its tiny arms.*

DESERT RICHES

The Gobi Desert, in the heart of Central Asia, is a harsh but spectacular region that attracts many fossil hunters. It contains huge deposits of rock dating back to the time of the dinosaurs, and because it lies so far from the sea, rainfall is very low, and much of the rock is bare. This is the kind of landscape where fossilized remains literally stick out of the ground. However, finding them needs sharp eyesight and dedication—particularly when the hot summer wind hurls stinging sand through the air.

During the 1920s the American Museum of Natural History mounted several large-scale

△ *The Bayn Dzag, or Flaming Cliffs, of southern Mongolia were laid down during the Cretaceous. The cliffs are being slowly eaten away by wind and sporadic desert storms.*

▷ *Using a pocket knife, a Mongolian paleontologist carefully chips away at the bedrock surrounding a fossilized* Protoceratops *skull revealed beneath the surface of the cliffs.*

expeditions to this isolated region, using trucks and camels to carry their supplies. Initially the aim was to unearth fossils of early humans, but none were found. However, other fossils were there in abundance. At a site known as the Bayn Dzak, or Flaming Cliffs, in southern Mongolia, one team discovered large numbers of fossilized eggs, and the remains of over 100 *Protoceratops*—animals that probably died after they and their eggs were buried by sand. These expeditions also uncovered remains of *Velociraptor* and *Oviraptor*, small predatory theropods.

During the Soviet Era the Gobi was closed to western scientists, but since Mongolia became independent in the early 1990s, entry to the area has become easier, and expeditions have been undertaken by experts from all over the world.

DEATH ON DUTY
Over the years dozens of species of dinosaur have been found in the Gobi, including heavyweight plant eaters such as *Saurolophus* and fearsome predators such as *Tarbosaurus*—a close relative of *Tyrannosaurus*, which rivaled it in size. Researchers have also found the fragmentary remains of several species of segnosaurs—mysterious dinosaurs unique to central Asia that may have been predators, plant eaters, or perhaps even a mixture of the two. As well as unearthing fossils that paint portraits of these extinct animals, paleontologists have also made some finds that show how they behaved.

One of the most famous of these fossils was found in 1923—an *Oviraptor* apparently smothered by sand while in the process of stealing another dinosaur's eggs. For several decades the egg thief's guilt seemed to be beyond doubt. But the accusation has turned out to be based on false evidence, because further fossils have been found. In one of

them the remains of a smashed egg include tiny *Oviraptor* bones. These show that the adult *Oviraptors* were actually incubating eggs of their own.

Together with fossils from other parts of the world, these finds have helped undermine the long-held idea that dinosaurs played little or no part in raising their young. Instead, *Oviraptor* seems to have been a devoted parent, doggedly remaining with its eggs, even when sandstorms threatened its life.

FOSSILS FROM THE FAR NORTH
Nineteen hundred miles (3,000km) north of the Gobi, the forests of Siberia flank the Arctic Circle. During the height of the last Ice Age, about 20,000 years ago, this area lay under a continental ice cap, but as the ice retreated the ground turned to tundra—a treeless landscape of low-growing plants that provided food for mammoths, woolly rhinos, and the so-called Irish elk. It was an icy version of today's African plains, with large herds of plant-eating mammals and predators such as wolves migrating with the seasons.

Compared to dinosaurs, these animals became extinct in the recent past: the last woolly mammoth, for example, may have been alive on Wrangel Island, off the northest coast of Siberia, just 6,000 years ago. As a result the fossilized remains of these creatures sometimes include traces of skin and hair, and in the case of deep-frozen animals (page 17), even flesh.

△ *In 1971 one expedition to the Gobi region unearthed something unique—a fossil of two dinosaurs that had both died while locked together in combat. The attacker was* Velociraptor, *and its intended victim was* Protoceratops. *In Mongolia this extraordinary relic from the dinosaur age has been designated a national treasure.*

◁ *Discovered in 1994, this* Oviraptor *was probably smothered by sand while sitting on its eggs. If the parent was cold-blooded, sitting on the eggs would have protected them against marauders, but if it was warm-blooded—as seems likely—incubation would have helped the eggs develop. From the fossil it is not possible to say whether the adult was male or female.*

▽ Two Chinese paleontologists examine a fossilized dinosaur egg in Hubei Province, in central China. Matching an egg to a particular dinosaur is very difficult. Instead, eggs—just like dinosaur tracks— are often given their own scientific names. Dinosaur eggs fetch high prices, and every year hundreds of Chinese eggs are smuggled abroad.

FOSSILS FROM THE EAST

During the 1920s paleontologists working at Zhoukoudian, in northeast China, discovered the remains of Peking Man, a human ancestor who lived over 400,000 years ago. As well as fossil bones and tools, the excavators also found deposits of ash deep inside caves—one of the earliest known examples of the deliberate use of fire. Peking Man was very similar to a modern human, but it belonged to a species called *Homo erectus* (page 216), which disappeared about 200,000 years ago.

Northern China is still an important area for fossil hunting today, but for many scientists the focus is not so much on the ancestors of our own species as on dinosaurs —and in particular, the ancestors of birds.

MILLION-YEAR-OLD EGGS

Some historians believe that dinosaur fossils, or "dragon bones," were known about in China over 2,000 years ago. But scientific fossil hunting did not begin in earnest until the

The history of fossil hunting is peppered with finds that later turn out to be fakes. People make fake fossils for several reasons: some enjoy fooling the experts, but others do it to make money. The fossil shown here is a particularly skillful one which was "unearthed" in China in 1997. Named Archaeoraptor liaoningensis, it looks like a link between feathered dinosaurs and flying birds. It convinced several leading paleontologists, and also National Geographic magazine, but on closer inspection, it turned out to be mixture of two different animals— a bird and a small theropod dinosaur.

1900s, when western paleontologists embarked on lengthy expeditions in search of animal remains. However, the people who worked on the fossils were not always from abroad. China had its own experts, foremost among them being Yang Zhong-jian (also known as C. C. Young). He studied fossils in Europe and North America before returning to China in the late 1920s.

Most of the early fossil hunting in China concentrated on the northwest of the country—the area that borders Mongolia and includes part of the Gobi Desert. Finds here have included a wide range of armored dinosaurs, which lived during Cretaceous times, and also a number of other large plant eaters. Among them were *Shantungosaurus* and *Tsintaosaurus*— two of the largest duck-billed dinosaurs,

▷ Watched by a large crowd, scientists work on an unusual find—a collection of fossilized eggs, together with dinosaur bones. If the bones and eggs are of the same age, this suggests that some disaster overtook the adult animal while it was at the nest.

or hadrosaurs—as well as *Tuojiangosaurus* and *Huayangosaurus*, two stegosaurs, both from the Jurassic, which were very different in size. The fossil-hunting expeditions also unearthed remains of *Mamenchisaurus*, a sauropod that was Asia's largest dinosaur and had a spectacularly long neck.

China has also proven to be a treasure trove for dinosaur nests and eggs. The nests include one find nearly 10 ft. (3m) across—a world record. There are some containing the remains of embryos, and others with more than 2 pints (1l) of rock-hard, fossilized yolk.

FEATHERED DINOSAURS

The first fossil to link dinosaurs and birds was *Archaeopteryx*, discovered in southern Germany in 1861. Although it was a bird, it clearly had some reptilian features, such as wing claws and a long, bony tail. But before birds like *Archaeopteryx* evolved, there must have been earlier forms that looked more like typical dinosaurs. In the last decade paleontologists sifting through layers of soft rock in Liaoning Province, northeast China, have helped fill in the missing links.

Sinosauropteryx, discovered in 1996, was one of these. A small theropod, or bipedal carnivore, it had strong back legs, but short arms ending in small clawed hands. It is certain that it could not fly, because it did not have even the beginnings of wings, but even so, its body was covered in downy plumage, which helped it keep warm (page 148).

Liaoning has produced several other fossils. Among them are *Protarchaeopteryx* and *Caudipteryx*, both found roughly a year after *Sinosauropteryx*, and also feathered, but flightless, theropods. These discoveries make it likely that, far from being unusual, feathers were common in small theropods and maybe other dinosaurs too, although unlike birds, these animals used them for insulation rather than for flight.

But why has this one part of China yielded

so many fossils of these feathered theropods? One reason is that, like southern Germany, this region was covered with shallow lakes and lagoons at the time when the ancestors of birds were alive. In southern Germany, *Archaeopteryx* probably crashed into the water and drowned, sinking to the bottom and becoming covered in fine silt. In Liaoning small feathered theropods probably fell in after a natural disaster, such as a volcanic eruption. As with *Archaeopteryx*, lake silt created superbly detailed fossils, which allow the outline of feathers to be seen today.

EARLY VERTEBRATES

Compared to feathered dinosaurs, tiny fish do not sound like the most exciting of fossil finds. But in 1999 Chinese researchers announced that they had found the fossils of two species over 500 million years old (page 30). This is an exciting breakthrough, because it pushes back the date when animals with backbones first appeared.

The finger-size fossils were found in Yunnan Province, in the far south of China. One of the animals, *Myllokunmingia*, had gill pouches and a saillike fin along its back; the other, *Haikouichthys*, was more slender and may have had slime-producing glands, like a modern hagfish. The search is now on for further finds of these ancient, but important animals.

△ *Sinosauropteryx was a feathered, but flightless, dinosaur that lived about 140 million years ago. It was unlikely to have been a direct ancestor of modern birds, but it shows some of the features that would have been present during the early stages of bird evolution.*

▽ *At 23 ft. (7m) long, Tuojiangosaurus was a stegosaur that lived in eastern Asia. China has produced a greater range of stegosaur fossil finds than anywhere else in the world.*

SOUNDS

TODAY'S REPTILES ARE LARGELY SILENT, BUT DINOSAURS MAY HAVE COMMUNICATED WITH GRUNTS AND ROARS THAT COULD BE HEARD FROM MANY MILES AWAY. THE EVIDENCE FOR THIS COMES LARGELY FROM THEIR SKULLS.

Animals use sound mainly to keep in touch and to ward off their rivals and enemies. For dinosaurs, particularly herd-forming plant eaters, this kind of communication could have been a valuable aid to survival. Periodic contact calls made by animals as they fed would have helped the herd stay together. Much louder alarm calls produced when a predator was spotted would let other herd members know that they were in imminent danger of attack. And for dinosaurs as a whole, far-reaching courtship calls would have allowed males to attract mates.

ECHOES FROM THE PAST
Animals make sounds in two different ways: by rubbing body parts together or by using their vocal cords to make air vibrate when they breathe. Most dinosaurs probably had vocal cords, but none have survived in fossils.

Other soft parts, such as cheeks and lips, modify the sound that is made, but few signs of these survive. Fossil skeletons do show the air spaces in the skull and the length of the trachea, or windpipe. As with wind instruments, the larger these are the deeper the sound that would be made.

If they did make sounds, the smallest dinosaurs, such as *Saltopus*, would probably have produced a high-pitched piping like birdsong. Giant sauropods would have made deep sounds too low for the human ear to hear. Each species would have had its own calls, and within each species individuals would have had their own distinctive voice.

COMPUTING A CALL
For sound specialists, hadrosaurs (pages 104–107) are particularly interesting, because their crests look as though they might have evolved partly as a way of producing calls. The crest contained extensions of the nasal tubes, leading from the nose to the lungs. In *Parasaurolophus* the tubes double back on themselves, a feature similar to the coiled airways of cranes.

In 1997 a group of American scientists used a medical scanner on a *Parasaurolophus* skull to identify the exact shape of the air passages which were preserved as solid rock. They were able to generate sounds that the dinosaur might have made. The result was a collection of low-pitched rumblings, the first dinosaur calls to be heard on Earth for over 65 million years.

▷ Parasaurolophus' *crest, with its trombonelike arrangement of airways, was a natural resonating chamber. In this artist's impression a male is calling by inflating his cheeks and blowing air out of his nose. The nostrils may have acted like valves, allowing it to alter the sound.*

THE MEAT EATERS

The theropods—a word that means "beast-footed"— were distant cousins of the sauropods (page 71), but their shape and way of life could hardly have been more different. Instead of walking slowly on all fours, most theropods ran on two, and they ate meat—not plants. This large and varied group of carnivores included some early species that were not much larger than a cat, as well as (later) the largest predators that have ever lived on dry land. Most giant theropods hunted alone, but the smaller species, described in this chapter, were smart killers that worked in packs.

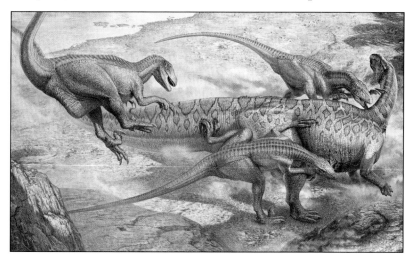

HUNTERS ON THE RUN
Sprinting across a Late Triassic landscape, a pack of Coelophysis *approach a cetiosaur feeding in the marshy shallows of a lake. They usually hunt much smaller prey, but the plant eater is at a disadvantage on the soft ground, and the pack may stand a chance of making a kill.*